Capitalism and Modernity

The nature of modernity, and its connection with capitalism, are questions at the forefront of contemporary sociological debate.

Derek Sayer re-examines the answers given by Karl Marx and Max Weber, authors of two of the most profound sociological critiques of modernity. His reassessment of Marx and Weber on capitalism and modernity provides a new reading which reveals the remarkable consonances between their sociologies of the modern condition. Going beyond the well-known stereotypes of 'the Marx–Weber debate', Professor Sayer shows that both Marx and Weber produced a challenging critique of the nature of power and subjectivity in modern society, a critique which retains all its intellectual force and moral relevance today.

A major work of original scholarship, *Capitalism and Modernity* is clearly and accessibly written. It is an authoritative and provocative commentary on a debate central to modern sociology and politics, and will be a key text in social theory for students of sociology, politics and philosophy.

Capitalism and Modernity

An excursus on Marx and Weber

Derek Sayer

London and New York

First published in 1991
by Routledge
11 New Fetter Lane, London EC4P 4EE

Simultaneously published in the USA and Canada
by Routledge
a division of Routledge, Chapman and Hall Inc.
29 West 35th Street, New York, NY 10001

Typeset by
NWL Editorial Services, Langport, Somerset, England

Printed and bound in Great Britain by
Cox & Wyman Ltd, Reading

British Library Cataloguing in Publication Data
Sayer, Derek
    Capitalism and modernity: an excursus on Marx and
    Weber.
    1. Capitalism. Theories of Weber, Max, 1864–1920
    compared with theories of Marx, Karl, 1818–1883
    I. Title
    330.1220922

Library of Congress Cataloging in Publication Data
Sayer, Derek.
    Capitalism and modernity: an excursus on Marx and
    Weber / Derek Sayer.
    p.   cm.
    Includes bibliographical references.
    1. Civilization, Modern. 2. Capitalism. 3. Marx, Karl,
    1818–1883 – Views on capitalism. 4. Weber, Max,
    1864–1920 – Views on capitalism. I. Title.
    HM101.S28145   1990
    306.3'42–dc20   90-8337

ISBN 0–415–01728–9

To Suzy, Lesley, Audrey, Jenny
and Natalie – and Virginia

Contents

Preface

To begin with what might appear to be a digression in a work of social theory, in a way which may or may not be apparent, events of 1989 in two central squares of capital cities frame what I try to say here. As I was close to finishing this book there came the 'tender revolution' (as the Czechs call it) whose most visible manifestation was the people congregating nightly in their hundreds of thousands in Wenceslas Square in Prague, to reclaim those who had long been officially erased from the national life and memory – the playwright Václav Havel, the gymnast Věra Čáslavská, the popsinger Marta Kubišová, and perhaps most poignantly of all, the minor forestry official Alexander Dubček. This was not the sort of revolution to which the modern world is used. It was, for once, a revolution against those *ersatz* gods of modernity who have stolen, by divine right of ideology, decades of people's lives, hopes and dreams; a refusal of the reduction of the personal to the political.

Informing this unusual revolution was (in Václav Havel's own words) 'a profound distrust of all generalizations, ideological platitudes, clichés, slogans [and] intellectual stereotypes', a distrust bred by forty years of experience. Havel (1989) drew a simple conclusion:

> The stifling pall of hollow words that has smothered us for so long has cultivated in us such a deep mistrust of the world of deceptive words that we are now better equipped than ever before to see the human world as it really is: a complex com-

munity of thousands of millions of unique, individual human beings, in whom hundreds of beautiful characteristics are matched by hundreds of faults and negative tendencies. They must never be lumped together into homogeneous masses beneath a welter of hollow clichés and sterile words and then *en bloc* – as 'classes', 'nations' or 'political forces' – extolled or denounced, loved or hated, maligned or glorified.

Such totalizing representations have been identified, in recent social theory, as critical components of power. They are by no means confined to socialism. In this book I argue that they are characteristic of modern sociality, and constitute its greatest threat to human life, what I have elsewhere called the violence of abstraction (1987). This violence is rooted in, but now goes far beyond, the capitalism which was modernity's progenitor. Its locus is the forms society and subjectivity take in the modern world. From this point of view we may be witnessing, in Eastern Europe, not the return of the prodigal to the fold of 'the West' hailed by politicians from Thatcher to Bush, but something quite new: a 'post-modern' revolution, if you will. I hope so. But to quote Havel again, if 'it is a long time since there were so many grounds for hoping that everything will turn out well', at the same time 'there have never been so many reasons for us to fear that, if everything went wrong, the catastrophe would be final'. He rehearses a dismal litany, 'from atomic war and ecological disaster to social and civilizational catastrophe – by which I mean the widening gulf between rich and poor individuals and nations'. Humanity remains poised on a knife-edge of survival.

Students played a major part in the tender revolution. But a few short months before, on the other side of the modern world, other students, equally courageous, had been less fortunate. As I was starting to write this book, they were brutally slaughtered in Tienanmen Square, Beijing, by a government which had commended itself to 'the West' by its pursuit of what it called 'the four modernizations'. These did not include the First Amendment. The events in the two squares were later to be brought together in a nice coincidence. We learned that President George Bush (having just vetoed a bill which would have permitted Chinese students in the USA to remain there after their visas had expired) had sent a high-level mission to Beijing to normalize US relations with the 'People's Republic' of China, on the same day on which that dean of normalizers, President Gustav Husák, announced his intention to resign his tenancy of Prague Castle. Neither in the 'West' nor in the 'East' can we yet congratulate ourselves on living in a post-modern world. The modern deities still demand their human sacrifices. There remains, then, reason to ponder sociological critiques of modernity. I try to explicate what remain two of the most profound (despite Marxism's substantial contribution to the twentieth-century ideological pantheon) in what follows.

I would like here to express my deep gratitude to those friends and colleagues who improved my efforts by freely giving of that most precious of modern commodities, their time. Philip Corrigan, Shmuel Eisenstadt, Raymond Morrow, P. A. Saram, Teodor Shanin and Bryan Turner read the manuscript of this book, in some cases through several drafts. All provided me with very helpful comments and suggestions, which I have done my best to respond to. To Alena I owe a great deal more than the translation of *něžná revoluce*, though that too is hers. It goes without saying that responsibility for not only the errors and omissions, but also the opinions expressed in this book, is mine alone.

University of Alberta
Edmonton, Canada
31 December 1989

Introduction

Capitalism has undoubtedly been a central preoccupation – in some ways *the* central preoccupation – of post-eighteenth century social theory. I have chosen here to interrogate the idea of capitalism through a detailed examination of the writings of the two men who were by common consent its greatest social theorists, Karl Marx and Max Weber. Capitalism is also approached from a particular standpoint: the degree to which its analysis is able to ground a sociology of modernity, understood as 'that which is "new" in "modern" society'. This nicely tautological definition, which I gratefully borrow from David Frisby (1985: 1), leaves open the question of just what this novelty comprises. Marx and Weber offer one kind of answer, to which capitalism, in different ways, is quite central. There have, of course, been others, above all those of Durkheim and Simmel. These contributions receive some attention here too, though much less than they deserve. I also try to connect, where relevant, with the concerns of more recent writers, notably Foucault. My main aim in this book, however, is to provide a clear account – if sometimes a critical one – of the sociology of capitalism and modernity developed by Marx and Weber themselves. It remains, I believe, supremely relevant to understanding the world in which we live.

For both of them, albeit in somewhat different ways, it is capitalism which is 'the most fateful force' (Weber) shaping the modern world, the 'general light' (Marx) in which it is bathed. For neither of them, I shall argue, is this proposition true in an economically deterministic sense. It is not that capitalism as a form of economy causes modernity to be as it is, though for both men capitalism's colonization of global economic life is a crucial agency of 'modernization'. Each comprehends capitalism, rather, as what Marx calls a 'mode of life'. Capitalism lies, in E. P. Thompson's felicitous phrase, at the centre of a 'nexus of relationship', a societal tapestry in which 'social and cultural phenomena do not trail after the economic at some remote remove' but are constitutive of what 'the economic' is (1965: 84). Bound up with capitalism are novel and distinctive forms of sociation, and embedded in these are new kinds of individual subjectivity. Wherever these may have originated historically, they form an essential part of what *bürgerliche Gesellschaft* – that German term which translates both as 'bourgeois society' and 'civil society' – comes to be. They also extend well beyond what is (mis)construed by most Marxists as capitalism's 'economic base' (Sayer 1987). One consequence of this, is to problematize the pretensions of socialism to represent a true emancipatory alternative. Instead it emerges as a perverted apotheosis of what is darkest in capitalism itself.

These forms of modern sociality include what is, for the first time in human history, conceivable as 'the economy', and its essential counterpart, 'the state'. Both rest on a radical transformation of the character of social relationships and the nature of social power, in brief, from what Marx called relations of personal dependency to relations which are 'impersonal' and mediated by 'things': money, bureaucracy. Class is the epitome of such a social relationship, and Marx and Weber concur on its essential modernity. The alienation involved here is the basis for that rationalization which Weber lamented as the 'iron cage' of the modern world. It is in the context of this transformation of sociality that much else in modernity takes on its saliency, including – again for both Marx and Weber – the domination of science and technology, the rule of law, and the pre-eminence of politics and ideology in what comes to be constituted as 'public' life. The 'private' sphere is comparably reordered, constructed as a privileged and represented as a primeval site of individual being.

Entailed in this reorganization of sociality is as far-reaching a transformation in the character of the subject: 'the individual', both public and private, as socially represented and empowered.

Underplayed or neglected in much commentary, this is a central concern of this book. The 'abstract individual' who is cuttingly analysed by Marx is the same creature whose existential isolation and moral *Angst* are so sympathetically addressed by Weber. Calculation as an orientation to conduct, and experience of 'society' as a mere external environment of individual action (which may become a means to personal ends), are fundamental to capitalism's 'mode of life'. So are new forms of self-discipline and a distinctive ethos of conduct, which constrain and empower modern individuals in fundamentally novel ways, regulating the most intimate reaches of their humanity. Indeed, I shall suggest, the very antinomy of 'individual' and 'society' which has been the locus of so many methodological debates in sociology may itself be understood as a uniquely modern perception.

This book is concerned not with the economics, but above all with this *sociology* of capitalism: the forms of sociation and subjectivity which it presupposes and provides the key vehicle of generalizing. I argue, against the drift of much interpretation, that what Marx and Weber agree upon in this realm of their work is a good deal more significant (and of greater importance for sociology) than what divides them, and provides a basis, perhaps, for going beyond both. I try to show this concurrence in detail, particularly in regard to class and bureaucracy. I hope this has not led me to minimize Marx's and Weber's differences, although I doubt this commentary is likely much to satisfy fundamentalists on either side. But through writing this book I have come to the conclusion that what is conventionally represented as 'The Marx–Weber Debate' simply misses the wood for the trees. I hope some readers will agree that, in this area, a rethinking of hackneyed textbook certainties is long overdue. Of course, what I argue here is not without precedent, and owes much to the earlier work of others, notably Karl Löwith's classic essay (1982); still, to my mind, the best study yet written on Marx and Weber.

There are certain issues not addressed here which I think need to be signalled at the outset. I do not discuss, except in passing, that matter on which Weber found (what he believed to be) Karl Marx's position least satisfactory, the question of the origins of capitalism. This is not a work of historiography. As Marx said, to write 'the real history' of capitalism is 'a work in its own right' – a work he did not, incidentally, undertake. For the record, I side with Weber, in his general approach if not always in his specific conclusions: I do not consider capitalism came into the world as a result of purely 'material' causes. But then I do not believe Marx seriously thought it did either. Here as elsewhere, it is wise to distinguish what Marx himself wrote from what his followers and critics have together made of him (Sayer 1987, 1989).

Also absent from this book is any serious consideration of the historical contexts in which Marx and Weber were themselves writing, and how these might have affected their ideas. But it needs to be remembered that Marx was born in 1818, three years after the Treaty of Vienna, while Weber was a man for whom the revolutions of 1848 were as distant as that of 1789. Born in 1864, he was a child of four when *Das Kapital* was published. Marx charts, and in many respects celebrates, modernity in the making. He died in 1883 – more than a century ago – confident of capitalism's essential transitoriness. Weber, who was to live through the civilized barbarism of World War One, speaks for the *fin de siècle*; a victorious capitalism, and a modern world grown familiar. One is tempted to say, misusing Marx's words in *The Communist Manifesto* (1848: 487), that Weber confronted modernity with 'sober senses'; and his was perhaps the first generation able to do so. He took it as an accomplished world order rather than a staging-post on the road to human self-fulfilment – and his response was profoundly ambivalent, rather than celebratory or apocalyptic. In some ways his critique of capitalism, as a life-denying force, is *more* trenchant than Marx's; unsurprisingly perhaps, because Weber lived to witness the enormous power of what for his predecessor was only beginning to take shape. He died in 1920, deeply pessimistic for the future. He greeted the Russian revolution, made – or usurped – in the name of Marxism, with foreboding. One consequence of his historical location was that his critique of modernity extended far beyond capitalism, to encompass 'rational socialism' as well.

Finally, I do not broach the question here of whether the modernity anatomized by Marx and Weber is *passé*, and I thereby ignore a major set of current debates. This book is influenced in its approach by 'post-modernist' literature, but the issue of post-modernity as a social state is not addressed in its pages. That does not mean I consider the subject unimportant. There are simply limits to what can reasonably be discussed in an essay of this length. That said, it seems to me that before we can treat of post-modernity we need a clear idea of what modernity itself is, and there remains, in the work of Marx and Weber, a wealth of insight into this condition which has not yet by any means been exhausted. A re-reading of both in the light of allegedly post-modern pre-occupations may be both timely and rewarding.

One last preliminary clarification is in order. It is now becoming common to translate the 'sexist' language of classical sociologists into something which is more acceptable for our emancipated times. In the part of the modern world where I live, women's wages stand at around 65 per cent of men's (and 44 per cent of the full-time 'labour force' is female), but gender-neutral language is *de rigueur*. Much as Kelly-Gadol argued 'there was no Renaissance for women – at least not during the Renaissance' (1977: 139), whether women (or, in fact, the great majority of the world's population) have experienced 'modernity' as construed by soci-ologists at all is more than debatable. I have left Marx's and Weber's words unsanitized, quite deliberately. That, for the most part, they universalize under the sign of the modern the social experience of *men* should, to my mind, be highlighted, not swept under a unisex linguistic carpet. When they say 'Man', that is pre-cisely who they usually mean. It is here, I believe, that all classical sociologies of modernity are most wanting, and their conceptions of capitalism least illuminating. To imagine this deficiency can be remedied by changing the gender of pronouns is to efface even more thoroughly that world of feminine experience sociology has so conspicuously neglected. It silences by a token inclusion, of a kind that Marx and Weber might recognize as paradigmatically modern (since they each unmask the same abstract universaliza-tion in other spheres of life). It is also, of course, patronizing in the extreme.

If the French Revolution were to recur eternally, French historians would be less proud of Robespierre. But because they deal
with something that will not return, the bloody years of the
Revolution have turned into mere words, theories, and discussions, have become lighter than feathers, frightening no one.
There is an infinite difference between a Robespierre who occurs only once in history and a Robespierre who eternally returns, chopping off French heads.

Let us therefore agree that the idea of eternal return implies
a perspective from which things appear other than as we know
them: they appear without the mitigating circumstance of their
transitory nature. This mitigating circumstance prevents us
from coming to a verdict. For how can we condemn something
that is ephemeral, in transit? In the sunset of dissolution, everything is illuminated by the aura of nostalgia, even the guillotine.

Milan Kundera, *The Unbearable Lightness of Being*

The State Jewish Museum is not confined to material from the
Old Jews' Town of Prague. While seeking to exterminate the
Jews the Nazis set out to develop the existing Jewish Museum,
then very small, into an 'Exotic Museum of an extinct race', and
during the period of Nazi occupation the collection grew to a
total of almost 200,000 items, with synagogues in Bohemia and
Moravia and elsewhere in Europe making compulsory contributions to this unique documentation of Jewish life and
faith.

Baedeker's Prague

Chapter one

Mors immortalis

> There is a continual movement of growth in productive forces,
> of destruction in social relations, of formation in ideas; the
> only immutable thing is the abstraction of movement – *mors
> immortalis*.
>
> Karl Marx, *The Poverty of Philosophy* (1847: 166)

1

Although the term did not by any means originate with him – its
first recorded use, according to the *Oxford English Dictionary*, was
in 1627 – it was Baudelaire who first gave vogue to the idea of
'modernity' in his essay *The Painter of Modern Life*, written in
1859–60. His definition is a celebrated one: 'modernity is that
which is ephemeral, fugitive, contingent'. Baudelaire himself
understood by modernity simply the quality of contemporaneity
or presentness; all enduring works of art, he sought to establish,
were so in part because of their ability to capture 'the stamp that
time imprints upon our perceptions', to 'extract the eternal from
the ephemeral'. In this sense 'every old-time painter had his own
modernity' (1986: 37–9). But the idea of modernity has since
taken on rather different connotations. It has come to define the
present in opposition to the past, to designate an epoch. Ephemerality, fugitiveness and contingency are no longer the attributes
of any present, but qualities thought specific to 'the modern
world', in contrast to all its predecessors.

This notion of modernity was anticipated by Karl Marx and

Friedrich Engels in *The Communist Manifesto*, a work written at the beginning of that 'Year of Revolutions', 1848, when *ancien régimes* momentarily looked set to crumble the length and breadth of Europe. 'Constant revolutionizing of production, uninterrupted disturbance of all social conditions, everlasting uncertainty and agitation distinguish the bourgeois epoch from all earlier ones', they proclaim. 'All fixed, fast-frozen relations ... are swept away, all new-formed ones become antiquated before they can ossify. All that is solid melts into air' (1848: 487). Marshall Berman had good reason to describe Marx as 'perhaps the first and greatest of modernists', and his *Manifesto* as 'the archetype of a century of modernist manifestos and movements to come' (1982: 129, 89; cf. Frisby 1985).

'During its rule of scarce one hundred years', the *Manifesto* continues, the bourgeoisie 'has created more massive and more colossal productive forces than have all preceding generations together'. 'It has accomplished wonders far surpassing Egyptian pyramids, Roman aqueducts, and Gothic cathedrals; it has conducted expeditions that put in the shade all former Exoduses of nations and crusades.' Change becomes the only constant of modern society: 'the bourgeoisie cannot exist without constantly revolutionizing the instruments of production, and thereby the relations of production, and with them the whole relations of society'. Such change is wholesale, leaving no walk of life, and no corner of the globe, untouched. Capitalism, says Marx, has 'put an end to all feudal, patriarchal, idyllic relations', and 'pitilessly torn asunder the motley feudal ties that bound man to his "natural superiors"'. It has 'drowned the most heavenly ecstasies of religious fervour, of chivalrous enthusiasm, of philistine sentimentalism, in the icy waters of egotistical calculation', and 'stripped of its halo every occupation hitherto honoured and looked up to with reverent awe'. It has 'torn away from the family its sentimental veil', 'created enormous cities', and 'rescued a considerable part of the population from the idiocy of rural life'. It has engendered the modern state – 'one nation, with one government, one code of laws, one national class-interest, one frontier and one customs-tariff' – yet 'given a cosmopolitan character to production and consumption in every country'. It 'draws all, even the most barbarian, nations into civilization [...] In one word, it creates a world after its own image' (1848: 486–9). This world, Marx leaves us in no doubt, is radically new.

The *Manifesto* paints in very broad brushstrokes, and Marx was to qualify many of these sweeping generalizations in other writings. His opinion of what he elsewhere called 'the great civilizing influence' of capital is more mixed than this passage suggests. None the less these sentences sharply bring out two central themes in his thinking on capitalism. The first is its utterly revolutionary character. The new world ushered in by capital, for Marx, is fundamentally different from *all* that has gone before. Capitalism's revolution is rapid, unprecedented, total and global, and it is the sheer comprehensiveness of this revolution which allows us sensibly to speak of modernity at all. Capitalism creates a qualitatively distinct kind of society from any of those which preceded it. 'Only the capitalist production of commodities', says *Capital*, 'revolutionizes ... the entire economic structure of society in a manner eclipsing all previous epochs' (1878: 37). It does so, moreover, continually. Where 'conservation of the old modes of production in unaltered form' was 'the first condition of existence for all earlier industrial classes', the bourgeoisie – for the first time in human history – makes its revolution permanent (1848: 487).

The second theme, however, is what makes Marx's treatment of modernity distinctive. A sense of the fundamental novelty of the world taking visible shape in the nineteenth century is in one way or another a staple of all 'classical' sociologies. It has become a commonplace that modern sociology was born of the convulsions symbolized by the French and Industrial Revolutions, although it might conversely be said that it is sociology's own conceptions of the newness of the modern world which render this Minervan account of its origins plausible in the first place. From the perspective of women's experience, for instance, 1789 might not so self-evidently figure as an epochal watershed. Be that as it may, modernity can be argued to be *the* object of enquiry which first grounded the establishment of sociology as an independent academic discipline. This is attested in the sharp contrasts – of, in sum, 'past' and 'present' – which undergird virtually all nineteenth and early twentieth-century sociological theories:

Durkheim's mechanical and organic solidarity, Tönnies' *Gemein-schaft* and *Gesellschaft*, Maine's status and contract, Spencer's military and industrial societies, Weber's traditionalism and rational-ization, Simmel's monetized and non-monetized economies. Typologies and theories grounded in the presumed radical dis-tinctiveness of modernity continue to be the stock-in-trade of sociological thought. A century later Anthony Giddens, ardent critic of nineteenth-century evolutionism though he is, remains in no doubt at all that 'the world in which we live today certainly differs more from that in which human beings have lived for the vast bulk of their history than whatever differences have separated human societies at any previous period' (1981: 165; cf. Sayer 1990) – a stupendous piece of modernist hubris (and one which begs the obvious question of who are the 'we' of and for whom he speaks). But where Marx is singular is in his insist-ence that what makes modernity modern is, first and foremost, capitalism itself.

Capital, for him, is the demiurge of the modern world. It is 'the general light tingeing all other colours and modifying them in its specific quality', 'a special ether determining the specific gravity of everything found in it', 'the economic power that dominates every-thing in modern society' (1857: 43–4). Capitalism *is* modernity, and modernity capitalism. 'It is only capital which creates bour-geois society', says the *Grundrisse*, and it is bourgeois society which makes 'all previous stages [of society] seem merely *local de-velopments* of humanity and *idolatry of nature*' (1858: 336–7). In the meeting in the market-place of the free labourer and the capi-talist, asserts *Capital*, is comprised 'a world's history' (1867a: 170). Indeed, claims *The German Ideology*, it is capitalism which 'pro-duced world history for the first time' (1846a: 73, cf. 49–51).

The grand themes of modern sociology – industrialization, ur-banization, secularization, rationalization, individualization, state formation – are all addressed by Marx; most of them indeed in the famous passage I have quoted from the *Manifesto*. So is the darker face of modernity: the ephemerality and insecurity of modern life, the disintegration of community and susceptibility of society to its ideological substitutes, the anomic isolation of the rootless indi-vidual, the 'disenchantment' of the world, the iron cage of an enveloping rationality in which means usurp ends. Marx's writings are not entirely free from a very modern nostalgia for what Peter Laslett (1973) has dubbed 'the world we have lost'. Marx understood this in terms of 'the originally not despotic ... but rather satisfying and agreeable bonds of the group, of the primitive community' (1881a: 39), and envisioned humanity's salvation as lying in 'the return of modern societies to the "archaic" type of communal property', adding that 'we should not, then, be too frightened by the word "archaic"' (1881b: 107). He was not alone in this hankering for an Arcadia: consider Emile Durkheim's proposals for resurrecting the medieval guild (1984, Preface to 2nd edition; 1957). There is, in fact, little in *fin de siècle* sociological analyses of modernity and its multiple ills that is not anticipated somewhere in Marx's voluminous writings.

The question is, to what extent can so wide-ranging an analysis of 'that which is "new" in "modern" society' be grounded in a theory of capitalism? Marx's is the most ambitious attempt to do this, and thus an appropriate starting-point for this enquiry. It is not too much to claim that later sociological reflections on the topic, Max Weber's included, amount to an extended debate with Marx's ghost.

2

Before examining Marx's account of capitalist society itself, it is worthwhile to consider his treatment of the past against which this brave new world is contrasted. He sharply berated those who sought mechanically to draw out of *Capital* a universal model of social development, prescriptive of 'the general course fatally imposed on all peoples' (1877: 136; cf. Shanin 1984, Sayer 1990). But this does not mean that he had no overarching vision of the course of human history. He did, and it is central to his work. He summarizes this vision in the *Grundrisse*, the first draft of *Capital* written in 1857–8:

> Relationships of personal dependence (which originally arise quite spontaneously) are the first forms of society, in which human productivity develops only to a limited extent and at isolated points. Personal independence based upon dependence

mediated by things is the second great form, and only in it is a system of general social exchange of matter, a system of universal relations, universal requirements and universal capacities, formed. Free individuality, based on the universal development of the individuals and the subordination of their communal, social productivity, which is their social possession, is the third stage. The second stage creates the conditions for the third.

(1858: 95)

The third stage is, of course, communism, the second stage – that of 'personal independence based upon dependence *mediated by things*' – capitalism. What I want to emphasize here, however, is that when reflecting upon the course of human history at this level of generality, Marx simply conflates as his 'first stage' *all* precapitalist social formations; and he regards these, nostalgia notwithstanding, as limited, and limiting, forms of human being.

Marx is at his most savagely modernist (and in retrospect shows himself up as a true Victorian) in his writing on 'Asia'. I apostrophize because the continent in question was in large part a figment of the European colonizing imagination, as Said (1979) has devastatingly shown. Orientalist clichés thoroughly permeate Marx's discourse, as they do that of most of the sources on whom he draws. Two infamous articles of 1853 are illustrative of his sentiments. 'Sickening as it must be to human feeling', he tells the readers of the *New York Daily Tribune*, to witness the disintegration of India's ancient village life at the hands of British capitalism,

we must not forget that these idyllic village-communities, inoffensive as they may appear, had always been the solid foundations of oriental despotism, that they restrained the human mind within the smallest possible compass, making it the unresisting tool of superstition, enslaving it beneath traditional rules, depriving it of all grandeur and historical energies. We must not forget the barbarian egotism which, concentrating on some miserable patch of land, had quietly witnessed the ruin of empires, the perpetuation of unspeakable cruelties, the massacre of the populations of large towns, with no other consideration bestowed upon them than on natural events, itself the

prey of any aggressor who deigned to notice it at all. We must
not forget that this undignified, stagnatory and vegetative life,
that this passive sort of existence evoked on the other part, in
contradistinction, wild, aimless, unbounded forces of destruction and rendered murder itself a religious rite in Hindostan.
We must not forget that these little communities were con-
taminated by distinctions of caste and by slavery, that they sub-
jugated man to external circumstances instead of elevating man
the sovereign of circumstances, that they transformed a self-
developing social state into never changing natural destiny, and
thus brought about a brutalizing worship of nature, exhibiting
its degradation in the fact that man, the sovereign of nature, fell
down on his knees in adoration of Kanuman, the monkey, and
Sabbala, the cow.

(1853a: 132)

'English interference ... produced the greatest, and to speak the
truth, the only *social* revolution ever heard of in Asia' (ibid.). For,
Marx asserts, 'Indian society has no history at all ... What we call
its history, is but the history of the successive intruders who
founded their empires on the passive basis of that unresisting and
unchanging society' (1853b: 217). History here means change,
progress (an equation Anthony Giddens has usefully criticized) –
and possessing a history is a prerogative of the western world.
Weber too was to explain modern capitalism by the supposed peculiarities of 'the occident', as we shall see. In Marx's imagery of
Asiatic passivity we catch an echo of a common sexualization of
'the West' and its dark and mysterious Other, which exists to be
possessed. Like John Donne's 'My America, my new-found land'
(a metaphor for his mistress's body), 'Asia' is passively feminine,
an object of conquest and desire, modernity thrusting, masculine,
erect.

This 'unchangeableness' of Asiatic society, according to *Capital*, stems from 'the simplicity of the organization for production
in these self-sufficing communities'. They are based on the 'possession in common of the land, on the blending of agriculture and
handicrafts, and on an unalterable division of labour'. 'Each [com-
munity] forms a compact whole producing all that it requires', and
– critically – 'the chief part of the products is destined for direct

use by the community itself, and does not take the form of a commodity'. We have here 'a specimen of the organization of the labour of society, in accordance with an approved and authoritative
plan', whose corollaries are 'an unchanging market' for products
and the conduct by each producer of 'all the operations of his handicraft in the traditional way'. There is 'entire exclusion of division
of labour in the workshop, or at all events a mere dwarf-like or
sporadic and accidental development of the same'. The hallmark
of such communities is simple reproduction; they 'constantly reproduce themselves in the same form, and when accidentally destroyed, spring up again on the same spot and with the same name'
(1867a: 357–8). Whenever population increases, a new community is simply founded on new land on the same lines as the old.
Reproduction is mitotic, not innovatory. Nature worship and
mindless traditionalism are but the expressions of this millennial
stasis. For modern capitalism, on the other hand, 'Christianity
with its *cultus* of abstract man, more especially in its bourgeois
developments, Protestantism, deism, etc., is the more fitting form
of religion' (1867a: 79), and, Marx clearly thinks, a much superior
one. Nature for him was something to be dominated, and 'nature
worship' a symbol of human degradation.

Now, this construction of 'Asiatic' society is clearly, in one
sense, an extreme. But it also operates for Marx as a kind of paradigm of all that capitalism is not, personifying the Other in terms
of whose negativity it is defined. The motifs of these passages
recur again and again in his depictions of pre-capitalist societies
in general. To the degree that the more 'developed' 'ancient' and
'Germanic' forms of community, the social bases respectively of
the ancient and feudal modes of production, which he discusses in
the *Grundrisse* (1858: 399–438), escape this regime of endless cy-
clicality, it is because their communal foundation has already
begun to disintegrate. 'Slavery and serfdom', he considers – social
relationships which emerge in ancient and feudal society respectively – remain 'the necessary and logical result of property based
on the community' (1858: 419–20). For Marx all pre-capitalist societies share, if to a greater or lesser degree, a common constella-
tion of economic and social characteristics. These define them *en
bloc* in their distinction from 'the modern world', and provide the

foil against which the novelty of modernity is established. Much the same array of features is ascribed to the 'pre-modern' era (if with differing emphases and explanations) by Simmel, Durkheim, Weber, Tönnies and many others.

In Marx's version of the world we have lost, either property is expressly communal or, where individuals do possess private property (in the means of production), they acquire it only in virtue of their membership of the community. An individual's 'relation to the objective conditions of his labour is mediated by his being a member of a community': thus *property ...* means belonging to a tribe (community)' (1858: 416). As it was for Tönnies, the pre-modern world is predicated in *Gemeinschaft*, community. Such property is not freely disposable, but hedged about with various 'political and social embellishments and associations' (1865a: 618). The modern appearance of property as a primordial, unmediated relation between individuals and things, Marx argues against Hegel, is 'a very recent product' (1865a: 615n). Save for slaves, individuals, within these relations, effectively possess their means of production, though they may not legally own them (if we can speak, in this context, of ownership at all). This is a critical difference from modern capitalism, and one which has an important corollary.

Here, Marx claims, 'surplus labour for the nominal owner of the land can only be extorted by [...] other than economic pressure'; 'appropriation of this surplus labour ... [has] its basis [in] the forcible domination of one section of society over another. There is, accordingly, direct slavery, serfdom or political dependence' (1865a: 790–1). *'Personal dependence* characterizes the social relations of production' themselves, and hence 'forms the groundwork of society' (1867a: 77). Within the pre-capitalist world 'the appropriation of another's *will* is presupposed in the relationship of dominion' (1858: 424). All 'ancient Asiatic and ancient forms of production', he therefore concludes, are 'founded either on the immature development of man individually, who has not yet severed the umbilical cord that unites him with his fellowmen in a primitive tribal community, or upon direct relations of subjection' (1867a: 79). From the post-Enlightenment humanistic standpoint which informs Marx's writing this is a savage indictment of the generic 'past'.

Marx's pre-capitalist world, like Durkheim's, is one in which individuality is little developed. In Durkheim's pre-modern 'mechanical solidarity' 'the individual ... does not belong to himself; he is literally a thing at the disposal of society'. Thus, 'the more primitive societies are, the more resemblances there are between the individuals from which they have been formed' (1984: 85, 88). For Marx likewise, 'individuals may appear great' but 'free and full development, either of the individual or society, is inconceivable' (1858: 411). That, here, he is referring to ancient Rome, where his 'umbilical cord', if not severed, was already much frayed, merely underlines the general point he is making. Within pre-capitalist societies individuals are wholly engulfed by the social relations which define them. Their subjectivities are inseparable from their social position: 'individuals, although their relationships appear more personal, only enter into relations with each other as individuals in a particular determination, as feudal lord and vassal, lord of the manor and serf, etc., or as members of castes, etc., or as members of an estate, etc.' (ibid.). It is therefore 'difference and *separation*' which constitute 'the *very existence* of the individual' (1843a: 81). There is no gap between who the individual is and how his or her subjectivity is publicly represented.

Given such social relationships, production moves within the fixed orbit of 'a given set of wants' (1867a: 235), met by known traditional expedients. Use value, not exchange value, determines how much of what will be produced by whom. Most production is for direct subsistence, whether of the individual or the community, and only the surplus (sometimes) becomes a commodity. Even in the case of surplus labour 'given wants' tend also to prevail, limiting its scope. For 'the Athenian [aristocrat], Etruscan theocrat, civis Romanus, Norman baron, American slaveholder, [or] Wallachian Boyard ... no boundless thirst for surplus labour arises from the nature of the production itself' (ibid.). This is in sharp contrast to capitalism, as Marx analyses it. Pre-capitalist societies are not driven by the making of money as an end in itself. Trading peoples, for instance the Phoenicians in the ancient world or the Jews in medieval Europe, exist only on their margins like, in an image which Marx repeatedly employs, the Gods in the Intermundia of Epicurus (1867a: 79; 1865a: 330). It is, on the contrary, only after 'general wealth, wealth as such, has been individualized as a particular thing' – money – that 'the quest for enrichment as such ... as distinct from the quest for particular wealth, e.g. the quest for clothes, weapons, jewelry, women, wine, etc., becomes possible' (1858: 155). The love of money is an eminently civilized vice, presupposing a certain abstraction.

In Marx's pre-capitalist world everything remains particular and concrete. Social relations are personalized. Neither labour nor wealth take on a general, abstract form: 'labour and its products ... take the shape, in the transactions of society, of services in kind and payments in kind'. There is nothing at all complicated or mystifying about such transactions: 'every serf knows that what he expends in the service of his lord, is a definite quantity of his own labour power' (1867a: 77). 'The economy' does not take on a life (or a vitality) of its own, bewildering to its participants, as in capitalism. Production and exchange, still enmeshed in personal relationships, remain subordinated to social control. It is exactly this factor, however – what Marx presents as the immediately human character of economic activities – which keeps pre-capitalist societies locked in their repetitive cycle of endless reproduction or at best very slow change. It is just because here 'the basis of development is the *reproduction of presupposed* relationships between the individual and his commune' that 'the development is from the outset a limited one' (1858: 410–11). These relations for the most part neither require nor permit much development of productivity, which is, for Marx, the wellspring of historical development and social change. Unlike in capitalism, there is no *systemic* imperative towards constant 'progress'. Economic life is subordinated to the maintenance of the social status quo. Similar kinds of argument are made by Weber (1983: Chapter 2) on the throttling of capitalism by bureaucracy in antiquity, and Braudel (1977: 71–4) on its failure both in China and in the world of Islam. In the latter case, Braudel says, the great merchants 'were devoured by political society'.

A passage in the *Grundrisse* goes to the heart of the matter. For the ancients, Marx observes, 'wealth does not appear as the purpose of production.... The inquiry is always about which form of property creates the best citizens.' At first sight, this 'old view

according to which man always appears ... as the end of production, seems very exalted when set against the modern world, in
which production is the end of man, and wealth the end of production'. Thus 'the childish world of antiquity appears as something
superior ... it *is* superior, wherever fixed shape, form and established limits are being looked for'. But what the ancient world offers is 'satisfaction from a narrow standpoint', 'traditional
satisfaction of existing needs and the reproduction of old ways of
life confined within long-established and complacently accepted
limits'. 'Man' may appear here to be the end of production, but it
is always 'man ... [in a] narrowly national, religious or political
determination', who is merely, and endlessly, reproduced (1858:
411–12).

The masculinity of Marx's vocabulary here should not pass un-
remarked. It is characteristic of his writing and his time; but it is
indeed a masculine world which his sociology largely describes.
This omission (or subsumption under purportedly human uni-
versals) of feminine experience has, I believe, deleterious conse-
qences for his theory of capitalism, to which we shall have occasion
to return on more than one occasion. But the relevant point here
is this. Capitalism may fetter human capacities, indeed it is for
Marx in many ways the acme of human oppression. But the world
which preceded it, for him, offers precious little to liberate. It is
the bourgeoisie, for all its 'philistine' odiousness, which 'has been
the first to show what man's activity can bring about'. 'What earlier century', asks the *Manifesto*, 'had even a presentiment that
such productive forces slumbered in the lap of social labour?'
(1848: 487, 489).

3

It is, I think, necessary to add one qualification to what I have argued so far. Marx's texts do not form a seamless web, and in the
course of forty years' writing he was known to amend his views.
There are, especially (but not exclusively) in his 'late' writings of
the mid-1870s onward, at least the beginnings of a counter-
discourse to that I have outlined. The best example of this is perhaps
to be found in the drafts of his 1881 letter to Vera Zasulich

(1881b), a discussion based in far wider reading on 'primitive communes' than the earlier sketch in the *Grundrisse*. This deals at length with the Russian peasant commune, the *mir* or *obshchina*, which Marx by now sees as a possible basis for a distinctive kind of socialism, allowing Russia the chance to bypass the 'fatal vicissitudes of the capitalist regime'. Here, a more nuanced picture of pre-capitalist social forms emerges.

Many of the old motifs are still there. Marx argues that the *obshchina* possesses 'primitive characteristics' which it must 'shake off' if it is 'to develop as an element of collective production on a national scale'. Among the various advantages which differentiate it from more 'primitive' variants as *the most recent type* of the archaic formation of society', are its having broken from 'the strong yet narrow tie' of 'the natural relationship of kinship of its members', the development, within it, of private property in houses and yards, and the periodic redistribution of communal land 'so that each farmer tilled on his own behalf the various fields allocated to him and individually appropriated its fruits'. All of these 'permit a development of individuality incompatible with conditions in the more primitive community'. And it is, Marx is quite emphatic, only the achievements of capitalism itself which open up the possibility of the *obshchina* becoming the basis for a new social order. Its future lies in 'huge-scale mechanized cultivation', something made possible by 'the contemporaneity of capitalist production in the West'. Among the 'debilitating features' of the Russian commune, he adds, is 'its isolation, the lack of connection between the lives of different communes', its nature as a *'localized microcosm'*, which provides the basis for 'despotism' – though he no longer sees this localism as 'an immanent or universal characteristic' of communal forms as such, nor qualifies such despotism as 'Asiatic'. But these themes are familiar enough; they serve to underline the extent to which the generic model of the pre-modern world (and of private property and individualization as the major agencies of its dissolution) remained central to Marx's thought, even in 1881.

What *is* new in 'late Marx' is an explicit repudiation of the inevitability of the dissolution of the 'primitive commune' – 'everything depends on the historical circumstances in which it is placed'

– and a very much more favourable evaluation of the positive contribution of its specifically collectivist element to humanity's development. What Marx would not have acknowledged previously is that 'the primitive communities had incomparably greater vitality than the Semitic, Greek, Roman and *a fortiori* the modern capitalist societies', or that the Germanic community provided 'the only focus of popular life and liberty throughout the Middle Ages'. This is not a portrait of stasis, nor yet of the simple confinement of human capacities. Teodor Shanin (1984) is therefore right to suggest that 'late Marx' contains the germs of a very different view of history, which acknowledges not only a plurality of different roads to modernity, but questions the inevitability and singularity of that destination itself.

I do not think, however, that any more can be claimed. Marx never explicitly reworked his overall vision of history on the basis of these late insights. It is the dichotomous contrast of (capitalist) modernity and the 'childish world' which preceded it that threads the *Grundrisse*, *Capital* and his other major works. Whatever his growing doubts, Marx remained a modernist to the end, impatient of those 'prophets facing backwards' who sought the salvation of 'civilization with all its evils' in 'digging up again from the rubbish' of the pre-capitalist past (1855b: 243–4).

4

Let us define capital, for the moment, simply as a sum of money invested with the expectation of a greater return. This already contains a distinction which is crucial to Marx's historical sociology. The simplest form of the circulation of commodities, he says, is C–M–C; a commodity is sold for money, to enable the purchase of some other commodity. 'Consumption, the satisfaction of wants, in one word, use-value' is the 'end and aim'. This formula depicts most exchanges in the pre-capitalist world, as Marx portrays it (whether accurately is another question, but one which is beyond the remit of this essay). The circulation of capital, however, is different: here the movement is M–C–M. Purchase of commodities is simply a means to the realization of (more) money: 'the circuit M–C–M [...] commences with money and ends with money. Its leading motive, and the goal that attracts it, is therefore mere exchange-value.' In this case, 'the value originally advanced ... adds to itself a *surplus value* or expands itself. It is this movement', says Marx, 'that converts it into capital' (1867a: 149–50).

Capital in this generic sense is old. What Marx calls the 'antediluvian' forms of merchants' capital and usurer's capital 'long precede the capitalist mode of production'. Merchants' capital, 'historically the oldest free state of existence of capital', requires 'no other conditions for its existence' than 'those necessary for the simple circulation of commodities and money' (1865a: 325). These are met in many societies where 'the great mass of the objects produced are intended for the immediate requirements of their producers', and 'social production is not yet by a long way dominated in its length and breadth by exchange value' (1867a: 170). Merchants' capital can accordingly exist on 'the basis of the primitive community, of slave production, of small peasant and petty bourgeois [production], or the capitalist basis' (1865a: 325). But its role in precapitalist societies is a marginal one. It forms the basis neither of economic life nor the social order.

The function of merchants' capital 'consists exclusively of promoting the exchange of commodities' (ibid.); its profits are made simply by buying cheap in order to sell dear. Merchants merely mediate between sellers and purchasers. This form of capital does not control production itself, the arena whose relations, for Marx, furnish 'the innermost secret, the hidden basis of the entire social structure' (1865a: 791). Merchants' capital is 'penned in the sphere of circulation' (1865a: 325). Marx allows that merchants' capital may impact back on the sphere of production, in that it 'tends to give production more and more the character of production for exchange-value and to turn products more and more into commodities' (1865a: 327) and 'thereby dissolves the old relationships' (1865a: 330). But, he argues, 'its development ... is incapable by itself of promoting and explaining the transition from one mode of production to another' (1865a: 327), indeed it may actively forestall change through institutionalizing monopolies and other restrictions on markets and productive innovation (1865a: 334–5). 'Whither this process of dissolution will lead ... does not depend on commerce, but on the character of the old mode of production itself' (1865a: 332). This issue is of paramount importance in debates about the origin of capitalism which are beyond the scope of this book (Braudel 1978; Hilton 1978; Aston and Philpin 1985). The critical point, for our purposes, is that there is, in Marx's view, neither a direct nor an inevitable line of descent from merchants' capital to capita*lism*. He argues much the same regarding usurer's capital, or money lent at interest (1865a: Chapter 36). Modern capitalism is not the simple offshoot of pre-modern trade or saving. Later Marxist historiography has overwhelmingly endorsed this conclusion; so did Max Weber.

Despite the presence of capital, then, in a variety of pre-capitalist societies, for Marx 'the historical conditions of ... existence' of modern capitalism 'are by no means given with the mere circulation of money and commodities' (1867a: 170). What, in that case, does distinguish capitalism – or as Marx more often (and with a good reason, in terms of his theory) calls it, the capitalist mode of production – from these earlier forms of capitalistic enterprise? The answer, in brief, is that modern capitalism involves the *generalized* production of commodities on the basis of *wage labour*. The two parts of this conception are intimately linked to one another. For Marx, it is

> only from the moment [when] there is a free sale, by the labourer himself, of labour-power as a commodity, that commodity production is generalized and becomes the typical form of production; it is only from then onwards that, from the first, every product is produced for sale and all wealth produced goes through the sphere of circulation. Only when and where wage-labour is its basis does commodity production impose itself upon society as a whole; but only then and there also does it unfold all its hidden potentialities.
>
> (1867a: 587; cf. 1866: 950–1)

Let me take these two key elements, commodity production and wage labour, in turn. Together they define what Marx regards as the *differentia specifica* of modern society.

5

Marx calls the commodity 'the economic cell-form' of bourgeois society, and describes money and capital as being only 'further developments' of this form (1867a: 8, 80n). Fundamental to the commodity is an opposition which I have severally employed, but without so far elaborating: the opposition of use value and exchange value. The commodity is a 'unity of [these] two aspects' (1858, Nicolaus ed., 881). Their distinction is critical to Marx's sociology of capitalism, and underpins his claims as to the radical modernity of *bürgerliche Gesellschaft*. Pre-capitalist societies, he thinks, are dominated by use value. In capitalism alone does wealth overwhelmingly assume the form of exchange-value, and only there is all economic activity mediated by this social form. Entailed in this, I shall argue in Chapter 2, is a profound revolution in human sociation and subjectivity.

A commodity, Marx says, is (ordinarily) a product of human labour. It meets human wants of one sort or another. Its use value consists in its capacity to meet these wants. Use value is therefore a qualitative thing – it is 'limited by the physical properties of a commodity [and] has no existence apart from that commodity' (1867a: 36). It is thus specific to each commodity: we cannot wash clothes in a Rolls Royce, or drive to work in a twin tub. It follows that considered as use values, commodities are incommensurable magnitudes; there can, for Marx, be no single measure of utility applicable to all commodities. The use value of any given commodity is inherently bound up with its concrete particularities. It is this qualitative incommensurability of commodities, their 'natural' differences, which motivates their exchange. People trade goods to satisfy particular and different needs. From the point of view of its use value a glass of water would be infinitely more valuable to a man stranded in the desert than the largest of diamonds.

In the process of exchange, however, all commodities *are* routinely compared and equated to one another: they have, in addition to a use value, an exchange value. The elementary form of this is barter: six chickens = one goat. In all developed systems of commodity exchange, exchange value finds its normal expression as a price. The exchange values of all commodities, relative to one another, are expressed in quantities of a single equivalent, money.

The price-tag on a given commodity tells us in what proportions it can exchange for every other commodity: how many units of commodity x would have to be sold in order to purchase commodity y or z. As exchange values, all commodities, notwithstanding their absolute qualitative incommensurability as use-values, are quantitatively equated in terms of a single and universal measure. The qualitative particularity of commodities is thoroughly extinguished; they are merely material embodiments of the abstract 'value' which is the ground of their comparison.

What, then, is this 'value' which finds its expression in exchange value or price? Or, to put it another way, what 'common something' do all commodities possess which permits them to be thus equated, as they routinely are on the market? Plainly, Marx reasons, this cannot be utility, since as use values commodities are precisely incommensurable. Commodities, he asserts, have only one common feature which allows their equation as values, a social rather than a natural property. This is that they are all products of human labour – of labour, he adds, in the abstract, considered solely as the mere expenditure of human labour-power, measured by its duration, irrespective of the concrete character of the work done. Just as commodities remain incommensurable as material use values, so it is only in abstraction from their particularities that different sorts of concrete labour can be quantitatively equated. Hence, Marx maintains, the value of commodities is simply a function of the abstract labour socially required for their production: 'the value of one commodity is to the value of any other, as the labour-time necessary for the production of the one is to that necessary for the production of the other. As values, all commodities are only definite masses of congealed labour-time' (1867a: 39–40). This, in brief, is the 'law of value' which for Marx governs the capitalist mode of production (albeit in practice in complex and mediated ways).

Capital's argument (1867a: Chapter 1) for labour being the 'substance of value', which I have just rehearsed, is somewhat formalistic and open to some obvious objections: Marx's 'common something' could be a mere metaphysical artefact, commodities could share some common property other than labour (such as their 'marginal utility' to their consumers). He offers a stronger justification for his labour theory of value elsewhere, in a letter of 1868 to Ludwig Kugelmann (1868a). This takes us to the heart of his analysis – the social relations of whose presence, he contends, the value form is but the manifestation on 'the surface of society':

> Every child knows that a nation which ceased to work, I will not say for a year, but even for a few weeks, would perish. Every child knows, too, that the volume of products corresponding to the different needs require different and quantitatively determined amounts of the total labour of society. That this *necessity* of the *distribution* of social labour in definite proportions cannot be done away with by a *particular form* of social production but can only change the *mode of its appearance* is self-evident. Natural laws cannot be abolished at all. What can change in historically different circumstances is only the *form* in which these laws assert themselves. And the form in which this proportional distribution of labour asserts itself, in a social system where the interconnectedness of social labour manifests itself through the *private exchange* of individual products of labour, is precisely the *exchange value* of these products.
>
> (1868a)

In any society, Marx is saying, reproduction must go on, and for this to occur, some proportionality of inputs and outputs must be maintained. Behind any distribution of goods lies a distribution of labour between different branches of production. Some such distribution of labour, in this very general sense, is clearly necessary to any society, a trans-historical imperative. But the forms this takes will vary historically, according to the social relations within which production and exchange take place.

In the pre-capitalist societies discussed earlier, for Marx, human needs are known, as is the range of use values required to satisfy them, and social labour inputs are directly planned (or traditionally allocated) with this end in mind. Such calculation as goes on is in terms of concrete kinds of labour, not labour in the abstract. But this does not occur in a system of generalized commodity production, because of the social division of labour – that is, the historically specific social relationships – upon which it is predicated.

Within commodity production, the distribution of labour is 'spontaneous' or anarchic, and labour is private; that is, it is carried out by producers who are independent of one another and subject to no overall social regulation. Labour is, precisely, divided. The 'legal expression' of this division is private property. Division of labour and private property are for Marx *'identical expressions*: in the one the same thing is asserted with reference to the activity as is affirmed in the other with reference to the product of the activity' (1846a: 46). In these conditions, individuals produce for unknown markets, and do not know whether or not their labour meets a consumption need in advance. As the letter to Kugelmann continues, 'the essence of bourgeois society consists precisely in this, that *a priori* there is no conscious social regulation of production. The rational and naturally necessary asserts itself only as a blindly working average' (1868a). Production is regulated neither consciously, nor socially, but through Adam Smith's 'invisible hand' of 'the market'.

I should make clear here that this is not to say that a *social* order in which markets can thus 'freely' operate is not extensively and continuously regulated. As we shall see, Marx, like Weber – and Adam Smith – knew very well that it was. For all of them state activities guaranteeing the rights of private property and freedom of private enterprise were fundamental to the possibility of capitalism. *Laissez-faire* requires definite institutional and, as Durkheim (1984) was to demonstrate in his analysis of the presuppositions of individual contracts, moral conditions, or in other words exists only within a particular societal nexus, that of *bürgerliche Gesellschaft*. It is in the 'economic' sphere thus socially constructed as independent that anarchy (or freedom) alone reigns.

Specifically, individuals only know whether or not their labour is socially necessary – or in other words, meets a demand – after it is done, according as to whether or not its product sells, and at what price. Where demand exceeds supply, which is to say that there is a shortage of labour in a given branch of production relative to existing social wants, prices rise. Where supply exceeds demand, there is an excess of labour, and they will fall. The (hypothetical) point at which supply and demand balance is that at which all labour is socially necessary, hence relative prices at this point – Marx's 'value', or the classical economists' 'natural price' – express the relative amounts of social labour required under the prevailing conditions for the production of the particular commodities in question. It is thus only through the price mechanism that concrete labour inputs are regulated, and prices are conversely but the abstract expression of this underlying distribution of social labour.

It is competition between autonomous producers which brings out 'the inherent laws of capitalist production, in the shape of external coercive laws having power over every individual capitalist' (1867a: 270), to ensure this outcome. The movements of capital in search of profits, on the basis of price changes, will allocate social labour between the different branches of production in a constant process of rough equilibriation to demand. Thus competition, Marx maintains, 'is nothing but the *inner nature of capital*, its essential character, manifested in and realized as the reciprocal action of many capitals upon each other.... Capital exists and can only exist as many capitals.' This is, we shall see, crucial to capitalism's unprecedented dynamism, its 'constant *March, march!*' (1858: 340–1).

It is, then, the social relations specific to commodity production – its division of social labour – which for Marx explain why labour inputs have thus to be expressed in the 'mystifying' form of exchange value, and value, conversely, is constituted by labour. He draws the contrast with pre-capitalist societies. 'The concept "value"', he argues, 'presupposes "exchanges" of the products. Where labour is communal, the relations of men in their social production do not manifest themselves as "values" of "things". Exchange of products as commodities is a method of exchanging labour, [it demonstrates] the dependence of the labour of each upon the labour of others [and corresponds to] a certain mode of social labour or social production' (1863, vol. 3: 129–30). It is 'the *social division of labour* [which] forms the foundation of all production of commodities' (1867a: 351). All products of labour, whatever the form of society, have a use value. But exchange value – the quality which distinguishes the commodity as a specific social form taken by the product of labour – only arises where this division of labour exists. Value is a property that objects acquire not from nature, but from a particular kind of society. Exchange value is the form in which 'the labour of the isolated individual' – the individual isolated by the division of labour – manifests itself 'as general, social labour' (1863, vol. 1: 207). This 'isolated individual' is a key figure in Marx's discourse, the ideal subject of the modern world.

6

For Marx, the dividing line between the various 'antediluvian' forms of capital, and capitalism, comes when capital takes over the process of production itself and transforms it into a mere vehicle of capital expansion. Basic to this, for a multiplicity of reasons, is wage labour, which is therefore the fundamental, and distinguishing, characteristic of the specifically capitalist mode of (commodity) production. Only on this foundation 'does the commodity actually become the *universal elementary form of wealth*', and 'only then can it be said that production has become the *production of commodities* throughout its entire length and breadth'. Only then is 'use value ... universally mediated by exchange value' (1866: 950–1). To comprehend why this is so, we need to probe behind the simple formula for the circulation of capital I gave above, M–C–M, or money which makes more money, and enquire into how, for Marx, this seemingly miraculous value expansion occurs.

Capitalists invest money in buying means of production and labour, which they employ to produce goods for selling on the market, goods whose sale yields a profit. I am speaking here of industrial capital: commercial and interest-bearing capital (the modern descendants of merchants' and usurer's capital) are for Marx parasitic upon this, deriving their profits from the surplus value actually created in the sphere of production. Marx assumes that all transactions here take place according to the law of value: in other words, that capitalists buy labour and means of production and sell their products at their value, as determined by labour-time. But this leads to a conundrum. If equivalents are exchanged throughout, whence comes the profit which is the aim of the whole procedure? How can a process in which all exchanges are of equal values furnish the capitalist with a surplus value?

Marx's solution – the so-called theory of surplus value – is an elegant, if contentious one. He divides the capitalist's investment into two categories, which he calls constant capital and variable capital. Constant capital is the outlay on means of production: plant, machinery, raw materials, fuels and so on. In so far as the labour involved in producing these is a part of the total labour necessary to the manufacture of the eventual product, the value of this constant capital is preserved as part of the value of that product. Variable capital is the outlay on labour: the wage bill. Wages purchase what Marx calls the labour-power of the worker; an individual's capacity to work during the period for which he or she is employed. Surplus value – profit – arises from the difference between the value of labour-power, and the value which is newly created when this power is used.

The value of labour-power (which Marx assumes that the capitalist pays) is determined in exactly the same way as that of any other commodity, by the labour-time socially necessary to produce it. Since labour-power resides in the person of the labourer, this amounts to the labour-time that is required to produce the subsistence of the worker for the time he or she is employed, that is, the labour contained in the goods the worker consumes during this period. Marx also includes costs of raising labourers' children, since they provide future labour-power. He thereby signals the importance of an issue he otherwise does not address, the dependence of the abstract labour which produces commodities upon the concrete labour which produces people; or to put it another way, the connection of the 'private sphere' of the commoditized capitalist economy with the still more private realm of household and family.

Here, the very existence of the working class has rested for much of capitalism's history upon a further, and an eminently gendered, division of social labour which Marx does *not* analyse but simply takes for granted or assumes to be in the process of dissolution as a mere pre-capitalist relic. It might be that an ideal-typical capitalism could fully commoditize child-rearing and housework, in which case this criticism would not apply. But historically it manifestly has not done so. In brief, capitalism has been abidingly patriarchal in both its dependency upon the unpaid and uncommoditized labour of women in the home, and its gendered organization of labour markets on this basis. This is one instance (among many) in which, as I intimated above, Marx's gender-blind conceptual framework blinds him to what has been, in his own terms, an essential production relation of capitalist society. Contrary to the *Manifesto*, it is simply not the case that 'differences of age and sex no longer have any distinctive social validity for the working class' (1848: 491). This form of patriarchy is not just a feudal 'survival'; it has been an axial principle of *bürgerliche Gesellschaft*, produced and reproduced as surely as the relation of capitalist and worker itself. This oversight, I suggest, is a fundamental one. For the implication is that many of Marx's key categories, like that of abstract labour, are at the least an insufficient basis for comprehending the complex of relations upon which production and exchange of commodities on the basis of wage labour – that is, capitalism – has actually rested historically. Not all of the essential relations of capitalist production assume the form of commodity exchanges, and those which do not have often enough proved to be conditions for those which do. Max Weber, as we shall see, takes us somewhat further into this hidden infrastructure. But for Marx it remains a virtual seraglio, impervious to his conceptual tools.

Subsistence is for Marx 'a product of historical development', and 'there enters into the determination of the value of labour power a historical and moral element' (1867a: 171). Wage levels are the object of class struggles. He also accepts that the expenses of education and training ('excessively small in the case of ordinary labour power') enter into the costs of producing the labourer, so that the values of different kinds of more or less skilled labour will vary. Marx's critical point, however, is this. The value of labour power is not at all the same thing as the value that is newly produced in the course of its utilization in the production process, as labour. It is the labour needed to *produce* the worker, not the labour that worker *does*, which determines the value of the wage. So long as the latter exceeds the former, then, value will be added, during the production process, to the capital initially invested.

Once set to work, workers are creating value. If their working day or week exceeds the labour-time embodied in their wage, they are creating surplus value: a value over and above the variable capital investment, for which they will receive no recompense. Together with the reproduced value of the variable capital, this surplus value will be embodied in the product, which the capitalist can then sell, at its value, and still make a profit. Profit can thus arise, consistently with the law of value. Its premiss is exploitation of labour. Profit – and thus capital itself, since profit is the source of its ever-renewed accumulation – is in the final analysis unpaid labour; and its magnitude depends 'all other circumstances remaining the same ... on *the ratio in which the working day is prolonged over and above that extent*, by working which the working man would only reproduce the value of his labouring power, or replace his wages' (1865b: 131).

Exactly as in his analysis of the commodity, Marx next goes on to enquire into the social relations which explain why this state of affairs should prevail. He does not, as I have said, explore the hidden infrastructure of family and household. For him two things are crucial. First, the means of production and subsistence must be the private property of the employer. This involves both the constitution of property *as* private – its disentangling from the community to become the freely disposable 'asset' of private individuals – and its concentration in the hands of one section of society. Marx seeks the origins of the former (a transformation commentators often neglect: see Sayer 1987: Chapter 3) in the section of the *Grundrisse* which deals with pre-capitalist economic formations, discussed above, and sketches the latter in Part 8 of volume 1 of *Capital*. Second, there must also exist a labour force, lacking in the means by which it could reproduce its own subsistence, available for hire. Without this, wealth cannot be turned into capital, since in Marx's analysis it is only the use of money to employ labour that allows it to be a source of surplus value. Labour power must in other words itself have become a commodity:

For the conversion of his money into capital ... the owner of money must meet in the market with the free labourer, free in the double sense, that as a free man he can dispose of his labour-power as his own commodity, and that on the other hand he has no other commodity for sale, is short of everything necessary for the realization of his labour-power.

(1867a: 169)

Capitalism, in fine, rests on a specific class relationship, and it is this which distinguishes it from all antecedent forms of simple commodity production. In Marx's words, 'the whole system of capitalist production is based on the fact that the workman sells his labour-power as a commodity' (1867a: 571).

'This relation', he observes, 'has no natural basis, nor is its historical basis one that is common to all historical periods' (1867a: 169). 'Free labour', in his twofold sense, had historically to be created. This evidently presupposes the destruction of all bonds of personal unfreedom, the side of things, he remarks, which is alone acknowledged by 'our bourgeois historians' (1867a: 715). But it equally (and for Marx above all) required 'the *Decomposition of the Original Union* existing between the Labouring Man and his Instruments of Labour' (1865b: 129) – a union common to all pre-capitalist societies, slavery apart, though in this case Marx asserts a different kind of union: slaves are themselves numbered among the instruments of labour. He sees 'the expropriation of the agricultural producer, of the peasant, from the soil' as 'the basis of the whole process' (1867a: 716). In Part 8 of *Capital*, he discusses how this occurred in England, the 'classic ground' of capitalism, focusing on 'the forcible means employed' (1867a: 8, 723). Disbanding of feudal retinues and eviction of customary tenants to turn arable land into sheep-walks, spoliation of church properties, enclosure Acts and clearances of estates are among the levers of 'primitive accumulation' with which he deals. Not abstinence, as preached in the 'insipid childishness' of Political Economy (1867a: 713), but violence lies at the origin of capital. It comes into the world 'dripping from head to toe, from every pore, with blood and dirt' (1867a: 760). It is 'conquest, enslavement, robbery, murder, briefly force' which 'play the great part' in 'the so-called primitive accumulation' (1867a: 714).

Marx is also categorical that state power was integral to the construction, and regulation, of this 'free' market in 'those physical and mental capabilities existing in a human being, which he exercises whenever he produces a use value' (1867a: 167). Not only, by the eighteenth century, had the law itself (in the shape of Parliamentary Acts of Enclosure) become 'the instrument of the theft of the people's land', but 'bloody legislation against the expropriated' had for several centuries previously penalized vagrancy, forcing the dispossessed 'onto the narrow path of the labour market' (1867a: 724, Chapter 28; 1858, Nicolaus ed., 507). Other laws extended the working day, regulated wages and labour mobility and criminalized workers' combinations. Marx also records (at some length) the 'external' use of state power in making the world 'modern', as 'the treasures captured outside Europe by undisguised looting, enslavement and murder, floated back to the mother country and were there turned into capital' (1867a: 753–4).

Like Weber (1966: 221–4), Marx did not see this looting as being the source of capitalism. To become capital, wealth acquired by such means supposed the employment of wage labour, whose origin was therefore the more fundamental question. He did, however, argue that colonial plunder constituted 'one of the principal elements in furthering the transition from feudal to capitalist mode of production' (1865a: 332, cf. 1867a: 756–7). In this sense, capitalism was, as Wallerstein (1974) and others have since elaborated, a 'world economy' from its very inception. As Marx himself expressed it, 'the rosy dawn of the era of capitalist production' was accompanied by 'the discovery of gold and silver in America, the extirpation, enslavement and entombment in mines of the aboriginal population, the beginning of the conquest and looting of the East Indies' and 'the turning of Africa into a warren for the commercial hunting of black-skins'. Following hard on this was 'the commercial war of the European nations, with the globe for a theatre'. This gives a rather different slant on capitalism's 'civilizing mission' than that familiar from the *Manifesto*. By the end of the seventeenth century, Marx maintains, in England the 'momenta of primitive accumulation' arrived at a 'systematical combination, embracing the colonies, the national debt, the modern mode of taxation, and the protectionist system'. All of these 'employ the power of the state, the concentrated and organized force of society, to hasten, hothouse fashion, the process of transformation of the feudal mode of production into the capitalist one, and to shorten the transition'. There is no need to 'bring the state back in' to Marx's account of the making of modernity. It was in at the beginning. 'Force', insists *Capital*, 'is itself an economic power' (1867a: 751).

This 'Decomposition' also had another consequence, which is equally indispensable to capitalism's generalization of the commodity form. It created, along with the worker, the consumer. Deprived of means of production of their own, workers came to depend upon the market as much for their subsistence as their employment. 'The events that transformed the small peasants into wage-labourers, and their means of subsistence and labour into material elements of capital', Marx points out, 'created, at the same time, a home-market for the latter'; and, he maintains, 'only [this] destruction of rural domestic industry can give the internal market of a country that extension and consistency which the capitalist mode of production requires' (1867a: 747–8). Previously markets were largely limited by upper-class 'luxury' consumption; most people did not meet their major subsistence needs through the purchase of commodities. They did not have to, since they were in a position, as households or communities, to produce most of what they consumed. Wage labour is thus as much a condition for the realization of surplus value as it is for its creation.

Here, once again, we catch sight of those other 'private spheres' which Marx neglects. Entailed in this separation of industry from household – of 'work' from 'home' – is a radical transformation of *both*. The constitution of the 'domestic' realm as one which is severed in space and time from the outside world of 'production' is a modern artefact, a product of capitalism. Consider, for a moment, how many of our everyday notions assume this topography: 'work' (that is, that activity which is waged), 'leisure', 'privacy', 'intimacy', 'family'. All have massively altered their meanings with the triumph of capitalism, with profound consequences for gender relations and identities. What is popularly (and erroneously) understood in present-day North America as the 'traditional' family of the male breadwinner with female and youthful dependants *presumes* commodity production on the basis of wage labour. This moral landscape is organized through regulated sexual identities, which it in turn provides models for thinking; an issue I shall return to in connection with Weber. To make myself clear, I am not asserting here that patriarchy as such is the invention of capitalism; like money and commodities (and the racism which capitalism has also made into a scaffolding of its own order), it is far older. Its modern forms, however, can be comprehended only in terms of capitalism's wider transformation of the social topography. Certainly, not all patriarchy is capitalist. But capitalism has so far been, amongst other things, a patriarchy, and integrally rather than merely incidentally so.

To summarize. Capital, Marx many times insists, *is* a social relation. Ordinary language notwithstanding, it is neither the mere sum of money the capitalist invests, nor yet the means of production he buys. These things do not in themselves have the capacity infinitely to expand their value. They acquire this fortunate attribute only through employing, and for Marx only through exploiting, wage labour. 'A cotton-spinning jenny is a machine for spinning cotton. It becomes *capital* only in certain relations' (1867a: 766; cf. 1865a: 814–15). Once in existence, these relations are endlessly reproduced. The worker constantly augments the value of capital, his products assuming the form of 'an alien power that dominates and exploits him'; 'on quitting the process, he is what he was on entering it, a source of wealth, but devoid of all means of making that wealth his own' (1867a: 570–1). 'He', of course, notwithstanding capitalism's modern domestication of women, is – and was, in the Satanic mills of England's green and pleasant land, long before Marx was writing – also she. The extent to which the early industrial revolution was made on the backs of women and their children needs underlining (Pinchbeck 1981); to be fair, it is documented in detail in *Capital*. 'This incessant reproduction, this perpetuation of the labourer', is, for Marx, 'the *sine qua non* of capitalist production' (1867a: 571), and the reproduction of 'this social relationship, this relationship of production, appears to be an even more important result of the process than its material results' (1858: 387).

If, then, it is the 'isolated individual' who is the ideal subject of the modern world, 'free' wage labour – and with this, I have suggested, the unfree, unwaged, and overwhelmingly female labour which makes wage labour possible – is its real social foundation.

7

Unlike in pre-capitalist societies, such reproduction is not mere replication. In Marx's phraseology, 'simple reproduction' gives way to 'extended reproduction'. As capitalism develops, it constantly revolutionizes both the material production processes and the social relations on which it rests. If it is competition between capitals – the consequence of division of labour – that impels this unrelenting dynamism, it is wage labour that allows this permanent revolution to go on.

In its first phase, which Marx terms Manufacture (and dates from the mid-sixteenth to the last third of the eighteenth century) capital transforms the social relations of production without, as yet, fundamentally altering the material forms of the production process itself. Formerly independent producers, peasants or artisans now work as wage labourers: in this sense 'the labour process is subsumed under capital (it is its *own* process) and the capitalist intervenes in the process as its director, manager'. The labour process has become, instead of the vehicle of the producers' own subsistence, 'the instrument of the valorization process, the process of the self-valorization of capital – the manufacture of surplus value' (1866: 1019). However, in itself 'this change does not imply a fundamental modification in the real nature of the labour process, the actual process of production. On the contrary, the fact is that capital subsumes the labour process as it finds it' (1866: 1021). '*Technologically speaking*, the *labour process* goes on as before, with the proviso that it is now *subordinated* to capital' (1866: 1026). Marx calls this the 'formal subordination' of labour to capital. It is, he says, the 'foundation' on which capitalism arises (1867a: 509–10), the 'premiss and precondition' of labour's subsequent 'real subordination' in Modern Industry (1866: 1026). This clear assertion of the priority of changes in social relations over technological development, incidentally, makes it abundantly clear that Marx's theory of capitalism is not a technological determinism, as has often been claimed both by (some) Marxists and (many of) Marx's critics.

Manufacture brings craft workers together in a single workshop, or at least, as in the putting-out system, under the authority of a single capitalist. This enables, amongst other things, the enforcement of greater labour discipline: 'the work may become more intensive, its duration may be extended, it may become more continuous or orderly under the eye of the watchful capitalist' (1866: 1021). Marx is as aware of the importance to capitalism of methodical calculation – he speaks of 'uniformity, regularity, order, and economy' (1867a: 503) – as Weber, and of surveillance as Foucault. Involved here is a revolution in the meanings of both work and time itself, whose extent (and whose violence) social historians have done much to uncover in recent years. In a classic essay E. P. Thompson (1967) has luminously explored the connections between work discipline, a new time consciousness, and Max Weber's internal Puritan clock. Work, Philippe Aries has argued, was simply of far less importance in pre-modern Europe; it neither consumed so much of people's time nor delineated their identities. Modern life, he contends, has become remorselessly squeezed between 'a laborious, hypertrophied professional activity and a demanding and exclusive family vocation' (1962: 71–3). Extension of the very hours which people work under the compulsion to produce surplus value is for Marx a fundamental imperative of capitalism. He points out that the statutory limit to the labour of children under 12 in nineteenth-century Massachusetts (12 hours) was the normal working day of 'able-bodied artisans, robust labourers, and athletic blacksmiths' in seventeenth-century England (1867a: 270–1). To develop 'a working class, which by education, tradition, habit, looks upon the conditions of [the capitalist] mode of production as self-evident laws of Nature' (1867a: 737) involved a wholesale (and strenuously resisted) cultural revolution, which embraced individuals' very subjectivities, reordering the social terms in which they were constrained to identify and value themselves and one another. Weber caught one dimension of this in his focus on capitalism's novel 'work ethic' – the moralization of labour, something despised by the privileged of many previous societies, as a good in itself. I shall have much more to say on this below. Suffice it to suggest here that such a moralization arguably presupposes Marx's abstraction of labour *sans phrase* (1857: 40–2); at the least it involves it.

Equally fundamentally, it is in Manufacture that production is given a co-operative form, and division of labour 'within the work-

shop' (as distinct from the wider social division of labour discussed above) develops. Co-operation, for Marx, is itself a productive force. Even without technical innovation, 'the effect of the
combined labour' found in the Manufacturer's workshop 'could
not be produced at all by isolated individual labour, or it could
only be produced by a great expenditure of time, or on a very
dwarfed scale' (1867a: 325–6). This too is a general characteristic
of capitalism. 'Co-operation', Marx says, 'ever constitutes the fundamental form of the capitalist mode of production' (1867a: 335),
and it remains the social basis for Modern Industry. Other than on
the foundation of 'combined labour', any large-scale application
of science and technology within the production process would be
inconceivable: 'it is only socialized labour that is capable of ap-
plying the *general* products of human development, such as math-
ematics, to the immediate process of production' (1866: 1024).
Marx sees this socialization of the productive process as capitalism's most important contribution to human development, although in its capitalist form it amounts to 'a refined and civilized
method of exploitation' (1867a: 364). Wage labour was again its
critical historical presupposition. Only the 'severance of the conditions of production, on the one hand, from the producers, on the
other' (1865a: 246) allowed the 'dwarfishness' inherent in individualized (or to be more accurate, in familial) production – the
peasant farm, the artisanal workshop – to be overcome. Capitalism is in this sense logically, as well as historically, antecedent to
the industrialism it has spawned.

The developed form co-operation takes in Manufacture is the
'detailed' division of labour in the workshop, of the sort that so
impressed Adam Smith observing the manufacture of pins. Here
crafts are broken down into their component operations, which
devolve on different individuals. Though Marx argues that this
specific form of division of labour is superseded with Modern Industry, once again the Manufacturing period lays a foundation for
modernity. In general, under capitalism, 'the developed division of
labour which appears *by chance* within society, and the capitalist
division of labour within the workshop, are things that mutually
condition one another'; 'anarchy in the social division of labour
and despotism in that of the workshop are mutual conditions the

one of the other' (1867a: 356). This is the obverse of the social regulation of labour and minimal division of labour in the workshop which Marx claimed complemented each other in the Asiatic commune, a combination which underpinned its 'millennial stagnation'. In capitalism, it is the competition stemming from the social division of labour which compels the specialization of labour (and therewith, its instruments) in the workshop, while such specialization in turn reacts back upon and develops the social division of labour itself. Entire firms, for instance, come to make components rather than finished products, something Marx remarks in Holland by the late seventeenth century.

Fragmentation of skills extends the subordination of labour to capital. Changes in the labour process *are* transformations of social relations (and of the identities of individuals). 'While simple co-operation leaves the mode of working by the individual for the most part unchanged', Marx contends, 'Manufacture thoroughly revolutionizes it, and seizes labour power by its very roots.' Previously it was simple dispossession of their means of production that forced workers into selling their labour power to capital. Now, 'labour power refuses its services unless it has been sold to capital. Its functions can be exercised only in an environment that exists in the workshop of the capitalist after the sale.' This 'creates new conditions for the lordship of capital over labour'. The labourer has now become 'a mere appendage of the capitalist's workshop', 'the automatic motor of a fractional operation'. This 'division of labour brands the manufacturing workman as the property of capital'. The 'intellectual potencies of the material process of production' – 'the knowledge, the judgement, the will, which, though in ever so small a degree, are practised by the independent peasant or handicraftsman' – meantime confront the worker as attributes of capital, 'the property of another, and a ruling power'.

To make capital 'rich in social productive power, each labourer must be made poor in individual productive powers'. Adam Smith's judgement, quoted by Marx, is worth recalling here: the detail labourer, Smith says, 'becomes as stupid and ignorant as it is possible for a human creature to become'. For Marx himself, this division of labour 'attacks the individual at the very roots of his life'. Manufacture inscribes the domination of capital in the very bodies of its workers. The detail labourer is a 'crippled monstrosity', 'his detail dexterity [forced] at the expense of a world of productive capabilities and instincts' (1867a: 360–3). 'Under the present system', Marx wrote in 1845,

> if a crooked spine, twisted limbs, a one-sided development of certain muscles, etc., makes you more capable of working (more productive), then your crooked spine, your twisted limbs, your one-sided muscular movement are a productive force. If your intellectual vacuity is more productive than your abundant intellectual activity, then your intellectual vacuity is a productive force.
>
> (1845: 285)

Weber was to echo this judgement. In the modern capitalist factory, he argues, 'the individual is shorn of his natural rhythm as determined by the structure of his organism; his psycho-physical apparatus is attuned to a new rhythm through a methodical specialization of separately functioning muscles' (1968: 38). The converse, of course, is the disembodiment of intellect.

None the less, Marx maintains, Manufacture remains 'an economic work of art' whose technical basis continues to be that of the old urban handicrafts and rural domestic industry. It was unable 'either to seize upon the production of society to its full extent, or to revolutionize that production to its very core' (1867a: 368). This revolution was accomplished only in Modern Industry, which materializes what in Manufacture is yet *in statu nascendi*.

8

Machinery is the foundation of Modern Industry, and Manufacture creates the conditions for its application by its specialization of labour and of tools. But by comparison with Manufacture, Modern Industry represents a quantum leap in both the development of productive power and the subordination of labour to capital. Where 'in simple co-operation, or even in that founded on division of labour, the suppression of the isolated, by the collective, workman still appears to be more or less accidental', machinery 'operates *only* by means of associated labour, or labour in common. Hence the co-operative character of the labour process is, in the latter case, a technical necessity dictated by the instrument of production itself' (1867a: 386). The social power of capital concurrently takes on a material form: 'the science, the gigantic physical forces, and the mass of labour that are embodied in the factory mechanism ... constitute the power of the "master"' (1867a: 423). With this 'real subordination of labour to capital a complete (and constantly repeated) revolution takes place in the mode of production, in the productivity of the workers and in the relations between workers and capitalists'. Real subordination of labour is the fount of capital's *mors immortalis*. Only now, Marx argues, in Modern Industry, does capitalism establish itself as a 'mode of production *sui generis*' (1866: 1035). It is with labour's real subordination to capital that we truly enter the modern world.

The imperative to accumulate, enforced by competition, is for Marx fundamental to capitalism throughout all of its phases. But with Modern Industry the form of accumulation changes. In Manufacture, the major form of surplus value was absolute surplus value; surplus value which arises from a simple extension of the length of the working day. Given 'a pre-existing mode of labour, i.e. an *established* development of the productive powers of labour and a mode of labour corresponding to this productive power', Marx maintains, 'this is the *sole* manner of producing surplus value'. But 'the specifically capitalist mode of production has yet other methods of exacting surplus value at its disposal' (1866: 1021). It is the production of what Marx calls relative surplus value which 'revolutionizes out and out the technical processes of labour, and the composition of society' (1867a: 510), decisively and irrevocably. It is this that gives birth to the specifically industrial society of modernity, and – in his view – lays down the social and material foundations for capitalism's supersession by a new mode of production, communism.

Relative surplus value arises not from extension of the working day, but from decreasing the proportion of that day which is devoted to reproducing the value of labour power. This can occur only if the labour-time socially necessary to produce the labourer's means of subsistence falls. Assuming constant real wages, productivity must rise, either in the industries producing items of workers' consumption, or in the industries which produce their means of production, for this to happen. For Marx, this does happen, and systematically, once machinery becomes the basis of production. Technological innovation can alone provide a consistent foundation for relative surplus value. The mechanism, once again, is the competition between capitals which follows from the capitalist form of social division of labour. In Marx's words *'relative surplus value* ... arises when the individual capitalist is spurred on to seize the *initiative* by the fact that value = the socially necessary labour time objectified in the product and that therefore *surplus value* is created for him as soon as the *individual* value of his product falls *below* its social value and can be sold accordingly at a price *above* its individual value' (1866: 1023–4). Technological innovation allows individual firms to derive a temporary market advantage because it enables them to produce in less than the prevailing socially necessary labour-time. However, this advantage is bound to be transitory: competitors must either follow suit, or go under. Either way, the socially necessary labour-time for the production of the commodities in question, and therefore their value, will eventually fall. This increases relative surplus value. But it also restores the *status quo ante* among capitalists, and thus the need for the whole cycle to begin again.

This relentless pressure to innovate is, for Marx, a secular trend of industrial capitalism, imposed competitively by capitals upon one another. He sees the ensuing growth of constant capital relative to variable (more money has to be invested in machinery and raw materials relative to wages) as the basis for a long-term tendency of the general rate of profit to fall, since profit is a function of the ratio of surplus value to total capital invested. This exacerbates the overall propensity of the system to crisis. Marxists have written reams on this; I would only note that Marx himself sees it only as a tendency, to which there are numerous offsetting factors (1865a, Part 3). Only an economically deterministic reading of Marx can give the falling rate of profit the centrality it has assumed in some Marxist literature. The social implications of accumulation via relative surplus value are as profound (and, I would suggest, of far more importance in Marx's prognoses as to

capitalism's future). One obvious one, which was much to preoc-
cupy Weber, was the growth of scientific rationality, with its ac-
companying divisions of mental and manual labour. For Marx this
was already foreshadowed in Manufacture, but reaches its apotheosis in Modern Industry 'which makes science a productive force
distinct from labour and presses it into the service of capital'
(1867a: 361). There are others too.

The production of relative surplus value leads to a process of
concentration and centralization of capital. Ever-increasing capital inputs are required to produce on the requisite scale and technological basis. Smaller enterprises, or those working with
antiquated technologies, are driven out of business or taken over.
Eventually the joint-stock company succeeds the individual capitalist and the family firm as the typical unit of production, and
capitalist economies become dominated by large corporations.
Notwithstanding the continuing private status of such property,
the actual process of production becomes increasingly socialized.
Within the individual enterprise, this enables (indeed compels)
the extension of principles of rational calculation and planning,
on the basis of that form of division of labour Weber was to call
bureaucratic management. For Marx this heightens capitalism's
endemic contradiction between 'anarchy' in the social division of
labour and (despotic) rationalization within each firm. He wryly
notes that apologists of capital can find no worse indictment of
socialism than that it would 'turn all society into one immense factory' (1867a: 356) – though thus to turn this charge against its
authors scarcely refutes it.

The destruction of domestic industry and the capitalization of
agriculture on the basis of mechanized production, are both, for
Marx, completed only with the emergence of Modern Industry,
with far-reaching consequences for society. Though he does not
explicitly make the point, this is also the completion of that
reshaping of the household, implicit in the wage relation itself, on
which I commented above. Therewith we have a new terrain on
which age and gender relations are reorganized. Urbanization,
and a revolution in means of communication – the 'shrinking of
space by time' – are equally the inescapable concomitants of
capitalism in its industrial form. 'Whole populations [are] con-

jured out of the ground', says the *Manifesto* (1848: 489). Marx observes that 'the whole economic history of society is summed up in the movement of [the] antithesis' between town and country, and elsewhere claims that this is 'the most important division of material and mental labour' (1867a: 352; 1846a: 64). Here again industrial capitalism represents a watershed in modes of life. The degree of its urbanization, which Marx, with his contempt for 'the idiocy of rural life', equated with civilization, is without historical precedent.

Simmel's (and Baudelaire's) metropolis – with its novel modes of being – is the *locus classicus* of modernity. David Frisby (1985: Chapter 1) has admirably expounded Simmel's acute phenomenology of metropolitan life. Simmel's urban denizen has close affinities with Marx's (and Weber's) 'isolated individual', who (as we shall see in more detail in Chapter 2) is estranged from the evermore extensive networks of social relationship upon which individual existence objectively comes to depend. This affinity should not surprise us, in so far as for Simmel it is 'the money economy [which] dominates the metropolis', and Marx's starting-point for his own analysis of modern subjectivity is precisely the exchange of commodities and the domination of the money form through which this is effected. The metropolis is for Simmel a thoroughly novel social space, combining unprecedented proximity (as in the crowd) and privatization (as in the naming of streets and the later numbering of each house within them). Constant interaction with strangers and a bombardment of stimuli fosters a social attitude of 'mutual reserve and indifference'; 'dissociation' becomes an 'elementary form of socialisation'. Marx too was to describe the relationship between capitalism's individuals as one of 'unconcern' and 'indifference' (1858: 100).

9

But he also remarks on another side to all this, and qualifies the heady modernist optimism of the *Manifesto*. By no means all of those related by capitalism inhabit its metropolitan centres; there are hinterlands too. Concentration and centralization on the one side, he points out, may entail peripheralization on the other. 'By ruining handicraft production in other countries', he argues, 'machinery forcibly converts them into fields for the supply of its raw material.... A new and international division of labour, a division suited to the requirements of the chief centres of Modern Industry springs up, and converts one part of the globe into a chiefly agricultural field of production, for supplying the other part which remains a chiefly industrial field' (1867a: 451). He exemplifies Ireland, 'crushed and reconverted into a purely agricultural land', its people 'forced to contribute cheap labour and cheap capital to building up "the great works of Britain"' (1867b: 142–3), as well as India, whose indigenous textile industry was forcibly destroyed by British colonialism. Where these sort of reservations are most apparent are in Marx's 'late' writings – not incidentally, those same texts in which he goes furthest in revising his earlier modernist dismissal of 'the past'.

A letter to Nicolai Danielson of 1879, for instance, offers a wholly negative assessment of the impact of the mushrooming of railroads within 'states where capitalism was confined to a few summits of society' like Russia. Here 'the railway creation has accelerated the social and political disintegration', becoming 'a new source of state indebtedness and grinding of the masses'. Its specific consequences included raising of taxes to finance state debts, inflation of prices of formerly cheap articles of consumption which were now exported, and above all a change in the character of 'the *production itself* ... to its *greater or minor suitableness for exportation*, while formerly it was adapted to its consumption *in loco*'. Here, he concludes, 'the financial, commercial, industrial superstructure, or rather the *facades* of the social edifice, looked ... like a satire upon the stagnant state of the bulk of production (the agricultural one) and the famine of producers' (1879). Capitalism in this instance is revolutionary only in the most destructive of ways. It creates what is then represented as a primeval stagnation. Marx here anticipates a large twentieth-century literature, from Lenin and Trotsky to Frank and Wallerstein, which sees the global spread of capitalism as engendering a hierarchical ordering of cores and peripheries in which the prosperity of the former and the poverty of the latter are two sides of a single coin. This world order arguably sustains that Orientalism which, in other contexts,

Marx himself unthinkingly replicates. Here, as elsewhere, his legacy is contradictory.

Such 'development', Marx recognized, often involves the reinforcement (or indeed the very creation) of supposedly 'pre-capitalist' social relationships and regimes of exploitation. The most obvious example of this discussed by him is slavery in the Americas. The cotton textile industry which pioneered the industrial revolution in Yorkshire and Lancashire, he points out, rested 'on the sovereignty of the slave-whip in Georgia and Alabama' (1861: 84–5; cf. 1867a: 443–4). 'Direct slavery', he had earlier remarked against Proudhon, 'is as much the pivot of bourgeois industry as machinery, credits, etc. Without slavery you have no cotton; without cotton you have no modern industry' (1847: 167). In *Capital* he draws a general conclusion: 'as soon as people, whose production still moves within the lower forms of slave-labour, corvée-labour, &c., are drawn into the whirlpool of an international market dominated by the capitalistic mode of production, the sale of products for export becoming their principal interest, the civilized horrors of over-work are grafted onto the barbaric horrors of slavery, serfdom, etc.'. These latter lose their former 'patriarchal character' and become elements in 'a calculated and calculating system' (1867a: 235–6) – a very Weberian opposition.

The 'requirements of the chief centres of Modern Industry', then, may not always be capital's creation of 'a world after its own image' – if, at least, the image in question is that of the 'modern', urban and industrial 'West'. Or to put it the other way around, capitalism embraces far more than what is normally taken to be 'modernity' (and an adequate conception of the latter ought to embrace the 'backwardness' *within* it). Wage labour may well be the basis upon which commodity production can alone be generalized, but given such a generalization it is not the sole source of profits to be made from buying and selling commodities. On the contrary, the global dominance of the capitalist market breathes new life into (and transforms) a variety of other modes of production, which adapt themselves to and become integral elements of the 'modern' world. The latter is thus a world whose modernity many of its inhabitants, strategic as they might be to the circuits of capital, have yet to experience. Plain slavery, serfdom, indentured labour, convict labour, sharecropping, and cash-crop peasant production have all at one time or another been component parts of the international capitalist order, if not of *bürgerliche Gesellschaft*. Nor are such phenomena by any means confined to what, by dint of this global structuring, we now name as the 'Third World'. Leaving aside the regulation of labour contracts in Victorian Britain until 1875 by Master and Servant Acts, what of 'guestworkers' in West Germany today, or Filipino nannies enserfed for room and board in middle-class North America (with the connivance of US and Canadian immigration authorities)? Frequently these divisions of 'free' and less-than-free labourers have been organized along ethnic or racial lines, a phenomenon which Marx commented upon in regard to Irish migrant labourers in England in the 1860s. Exactly as with gender, such differential classifications by 'race' have historically been as much a part of the capitalist epoch as the 'modernity' which they buttress, providing the living images of its supposedly primeval Other by which 'we' measure and celebrate our civility (Corrigan 1977).

This is not the only instance in which Marx's own analysis shows 'pre-capitalist' relations to be alive and well in the 'modern world'. He remarks, for instance, that 'with the growing productivity of capital, i.e. of the labourers, it imitates the retainer system of the feudal lords'. In 1851, that *annus mirabilis* in which Great Britain exhibited its modernity to the admiring world at the Crystal Palace, the total number of factory employees in the United Kingdom was 775,534, while the number of female domestic servants in England alone exceeded one million. Commenting on this statistic, Marx writes sourly that 'what a convenient arrangement it is that makes a factory girl to sweat twelve hours in a factory, so that the factory proprietor, with a part of her unpaid labour, can take into his personal service her sister as maid, her brother as groom and her cousin as soldier or policeman' (1863, vol. 1: 200–1). What he does not do is to consider whether, in the light of these figures, his generic contrasts of past and present perhaps need nuancing. Nor does he allow such 'anomalies' to affect his prognosis for the long-term outcomes of capitalism's development. Whether, more than a century on, we can afford to be quite so sanguine is dubious.

10

Marx himself saw the heart of the capitalist drama as lying in the way that the concentration and centralization of capital restructures his two core classes of capitalist society, and it is in this dynamic that the roots of modern socialism are to be found. For him, the ranks of the proletariat constantly swell as peasants, artisans, and the owners of small enterprises, unable to compete, are driven out of the market-place. Society is polarized as the wealth of 'dead labour' grows in proportion to living labour's poverty. Classes whose very existence rests on pre-capitalist modes of production disappear, and wage labour becomes the norm for the overwhelming majority of the employed population. Where the prevailing form of surplus value is relative, increasing exploitation is quite compatible with a rising real standard of living, as Marx himself acknowledges. But another concomitant of capitalism's repeated technological revolutions (and cyclical crises) is the incessant production of what he calls a 'relative surplus population'. This forms a 'reserve army of labour', inhaled and exhaled with the industrial cycle; it also puts a continuing downward pressure on the wages of the employed. This reserve army is for Marx 'the pivot on which the law of supply and demand of labour works', confining 'the field of action of this law within the limits absolutely convenient to the activity of exploitation and to the domination of capital' (1867a: 639). Hence 'the accumulation of wealth at one pole is ... at the same time accumulation of misery, agony of toil, slavery, ignorance, brutality, mental degredation, at the opposite pole'. This is *the absolute general law of capitalist accumulation*' (1867a: 644–5). It is a significant phrase; Marx rarely talks of 'absolute laws' of any sort. In capitalism, at least, the poor are always with us, floating, latent, stagnant, and 'dangerous' (1867a: 640ff.).

Modern industry brings other changes in the composition of the working class too. Mechanization destroys the detailed craft hierarchy of Manufacture: 'there steps, in the automatic factory, a tendency to equalize and reduce to one and the same level the work that has to be done by the minders of the machines' (1867a: 420). What Braverman (1974) and others call 'deskilling' is central to capitalist production in its industrial phase, and simultaneously a means of increased productivity and increased managerial con-

trol. 'Real subordination' of labour to capital extends the appropriation not merely of labour's means of production, but also of its
knowledge and skills, already foreshadowed in the detail division
of labour found within Manufacture. In every capitalist production process 'it is not the workman that employs the instruments
of labour, but the instruments of labour that employ the workman. But it is only in the factory system that this inversion for the
first time acquires technical and palpable reality' (1867a: 423). Abstract labour, Marx argues, indeed becomes a concrete experience
in modern industry: 'individuals equally pass from one kind of labour to another, the particular kind of labour being accidental to
them and therefore indifferent. Labour, not only as a category but
in reality, has become here a means to create wealth in general',
ceasing 'to be tied with the individuals in any particularity' (1857:
41). Increasingly the substantive character of their labour
becomes incidental to individuals, a mere means to the end of consumption rather than an affirmation of self or humanity. Marx famously analysed the deep alienation of workers from what he
regarded as the core of human 'species being' – the need and capacity actively to create – in his 1844 'Paris Manuscripts' (1844).
The analysis of 'real subordination' in *Capital*, the product of another twenty years of reading and thought, places this diagnosis on
much more solid historical foundations, but without, in my view at
least, at all altering his perspective.

Under these conditions, he thought, the working class would
increasingly become a class 'for itself', united and conscious of its
common interests. The concentration and centralization of capital is at the same time concentration and centralization of labour.
With it grows 'the revolt of the working-class, a class always increasing in numbers, and disciplined, united, organized by the very
mechanism of the process of capitalist production itself' (1867a:
763). Capitalism's workers are 'new-fangled men' (once again, I
think, Marx did mean men), who are 'as much the invention of
modern time as machinery itself' (1856: 656). Concentrated in
great cities and enormous plants, habituated to co-operative
endeavour, they epitomize modernity. They are the social class in
whom the potentialities brought into being, yet frustrated, by
capitalism are embodied, the harbingers of a new social order. 'By

creating the inexhaustible productive powers of modern industry', Marx wrote in 1854, the English working classes have 'fulfilled the first condition of the emancipation of Labour'. They have 'called into life the material means of ennobling labour itself, and of multiplying its fruits to such a degree as to make general abundance possible'. All that remains is 'to free those wealth-producing powers from the infamous shackles of monopoly, and subject them to the joint control of the producers, who, till now, allowed the very products of their hands to turn against them and be transformed into as many instruments of their own subjugation'. 'The labouring classes have conquered nature; they have now to conquer man' (1854: 58). Communism is for Marx implicit in the potentialities conjured into being by capitalism itself. It is 'the *real* movement which abolishes the existing state of things', whose conditions 'result from the now existing premise' (1846a: 49).

On the side of the capitalists too, concentration and centralization bring major changes. The joint-stock company has 'an increasing tendency to separate [the] work of management ... from the ownership of capital'; 'only the functionary remains and the capitalist disappears as superfluous from the production process' (1865a: 388). Marx anticipated some of his critics here in himself faulting Ricardo for failing to acknowledge 'the constantly growing number of the middle classes, those who stand between the workman on the one hand and the capitalist and landlord on the other' (1863, vol. 2: 573) – a recognition not entirely compatible with his overall expectations of class polarization. In the last chapter of *Capital* 3 he says that such 'middle and intermediate strata ... obliterate lines of demarcation everywhere' (and *more* so in cities, those heartlands of modernity, than in the countryside) (1865a: 885). This text was written, incidentally, at the latest in 1865, two years before *Capital* 1 went to press; it does not, as some have supposed, represent 'late' second thoughts. Such a state of affairs is ridden with contradiction. In one sense the modern joint-stock company represents a further socialization of the production process. It is in this sense, Marx writes, 'the abolition of capital as private property within the framework of capitalist production itself' (1865a: 436). But at the same time the flotation of share rights has the perverse effect of once more freeing capital from so direct an involvement in production as was found in earlier phases of capitalist development. The capital owner becomes a 'mere money capitalist', as parasitic upon the direct production process as a feudal lord. More accurately, there is now a plurality of owners, none of whose interests is any longer intrinsically bound up with the fate of any particular productive enterprise. Their relationship to the material production upon which their incomes ultimately depend has also become wholly abstract. There emerges 'a new financial aristocracy', of 'promoters, speculators and simply nominal directors' (1865a: 438); a class, and a form of capitalism often in conflict with the interests of industrial, productive capital. Max Weber too regarded this as a 'substantive irrationality' of developed capitalism (1964: 249; 1978b: 259–60).

Finally, for Marx, the production of relative surplus value gives an enormous impetus to the globalization of the market. Surplus value, whether relative or absolute, is only realized through the sale of the products in which it is embodied. As its magnitude grows, so too must the market. Once again the process is contradictory and crisis-ridden. Overproduction relative to effective demand, and thus a periodic failure to realize surplus value, is inherent in capitalism's 'anarchy' and basic to its 'business' cycles, and as I have indicated, Marx to some degree anticipated modern analyses of 'dependent development' and the restrictions upon consumption which it entails. This said, the realization of absolute surplus value 'is conditional upon the expansion, indeed upon the constant expansion, of the periphery of circulation', for 'the *surplus value* produced at one point requires the production of surplus value at *another* point, for which it may be exchanged'. This means that 'capital tends to generate more surplus labour as a complement to itself; *au fond*, that it tends to propagate production based on capital.... The tendency to create the *world market* is inherent directly in the concept of capital itself' (1858: 334–5). It is in this sense that with the advent of capitalism human history becomes, for the first time, truly global. As the *Manifesto* expresses it – in an image whose racism illustrates the Eurocentric vantage-point from which this universality is claimed – 'the cheap prices of its commodities are the heavy artillery with which [the bourgeoisie] batters down all Chinese walls, forcing the barbarians' obstinate hatred of foreigners to capitulate' (1848: 488; cf. Weber 1949: 58–9 for similar imagery).

With the era of relative surplus value, this creation of market relations takes a further leap forward. Now, markets are not just quantitatively but also qualitatively extended. Every increase in productivity, Marx points out, frees capital (and the labour it employs) for further investment. If relative surplus value is to be realized, consumption must not only be broadened but also deepened. The production of relative surplus value enlarges 'the sphere of consumption within circulation' through 'quantitative increase in existing consumption', 'creation of new needs by the propagation of existing ones over a wider area' and – most consequentially – 'production of *new* needs and discovery and creation of new use values'. Here Marx waxes lyrical:

> Hence the exploration of the whole of nature in order to discover new useful properties of things; the universal exchange of the products coming from the most diverse climates and lands; new (artificial) modes of processing natural objects to give them new use values.... The all-round exploration of the earth to discover both new useful objects and new uses for old objects, such as their use as raw materials, etc.; hence the development of the natural sciences to their highest point; the discovery, creation and satisfaction of new needs arising from society itself; cultivating all the qualities of social man and producing him in a form as rich as possible in needs because rich in qualities and relations – producing man as the most total and universal product possible ...
>
> (1858: 336)

Herein lies capitalism's enormous contribution to human welfare, its 'great civilizing influence' (ibid.). A more cynical view (I write in a city which boasts the largest shopping mall in the world, purveying, among other spectacles, properly antiqued life-size replicas of Columbus's flagship and Bourbon Street in New Orleans) has been well expressed by David Levine:

> it is the genius of modern capitalism that producers must also be consumers, and in precisely this way the fetters of production have been replaced by those of consumption. Most mem-

bers of modern society, like Gulliver awakening in Lilliput, have been tied to the consumer economy by a thousand tiny chains.

(1989: 106)

Other twentieth-century writers, from Veblen to Benjamin, have rightly made much of this critical dimension of capitalism's power, which binds agents to structure as private individuals (and members of families which have been reconstituted as units of consumption). We undoubtedly need a social psychology of consumption to complement Marx's focus on production, and there have recently been welcome moves in this direction (see, for example, Campbell 1987). Marx, however, can hardly be faulted for not foreseeing the Visa Card.

His belief, more than a century ago, was that capitalism had already become the 'greatest barrier' standing in the way of 'the universality for which [it] constantly strives', and this becomes the more apparent the more it develops. It is chronically unable to realize its apparent promise, because of the social relations – of private property and wage labour – upon which it continues to rest. Once a truly revolutionary force, capitalism has played out its historical part. Its violence and exploitation have swept away the detritus of the 'childish world' of the past, forcibly unified humanity in a single destiny, and opened up for the first time the possibility of a new form of society which allows the full development of individuals' capacities on the basis of their free and universal association. Increasingly 'it is, in a word, the development of the social individual which appears as the great foundation-stone of production and of wealth'. In the face of this, 'the theft of alien labour-time, upon which the present wealth is based, appears as a miserable foundation'. Capitalism has brought into existence unimagined forces of production and an unprecedented globalization of social relations. These 'two different sides of the development of the social individual', 'which appear to capital as mere means, and are merely means for it to produce on its limited foundation', now furnish 'the material conditions to blow this foundation sky-high' (1858: Nicolaus ed., 705–6). With capitalism ends 'the prehistory of human society' (1859).

Chapter two

Power and the subject

An appalling-looking man enters and looks at himself in a mirror.

'Why do you look at yourself in the glass, since the sight of your reflection can only be painful to you?'

The appalling-looking man replies: 'Sir, according to the immortal principles of '89, all men are equal before the law; therefore I have the right to look at myself in the glass; with pleasure or pain, that is an entirely personal matter.'

In respect of common sense, I was certainly right; but from the point of view of the law, he was not wrong.

Charles Baudelaire, 'The Mirror' (1970: 83)

1

I want now to move into less well-charted territory. In brief, I shall suggest that for Marx capitalism entailed – or was – a revolution in what might without any exaggeration be called the elementary forms of social life: individuality, relationship and community. It is a mistake, however, to understand this in terms of 'economic determinism'. Marx is arguing, not that capitalism causes distinctively modern forms of sociation to arise, but that it is itself a distinctively modern form of sociation. A 'mode of production', he wrote in *The German Ideology*, is for him far more than merely 'the reproduction of the physical existence of [...] individuals. Rather it is a definite form of activity of these individuals, a definite form of expressing their life, a definite *mode of life* on their part' (and 'as individuals express their life, so they are') (1846a: 31). Such is capitalism, and its making involved a cultural revolution – a revolution in human sociality and subjectivity – in the broadest of senses.

Focusing on this, far less often discussed, dimension of Marx's theory of capitalism brings us closer to the concerns of that generation of *fin de siècle* social theorists whose members included Durkheim, Simmel, Tönnies and Weber. There are many more affinities here than many commentators on both sides have been willing to acknowledge; not least, I suspect, because in the United States *fin de siècle* sociology has been co-opted for the war against communism, doing enormous violence to its trenchant critique of capitalism in the process. These affinities may prove to be among the more enduring elements in Marx's legacy; in some respects, indeed, he anticipated what are nowadays heralded as distinctly 'post-modern' preoccupations. They also represent what is in some ways a counter-text to that outlined in Chapter 1, and one which is subversive of some of its more apocalyptic conclusions. Where the centre-piece there was capitalism's hidden infrastructure of class relations, the *Leitmotif* here is the *Erscheinungsformen*, the forms of appearance, in which we experience modernity as subjects.

To begin (as Marx says we ought) with the 'real living individual' (1846a: 31). In the pre-capitalist world, as we have seen, for him there were no individuals in the abstract, only 'individuals in a particular determination' (1858: 100), whose identities are given with their position within a community. As more generally, things here are concrete and particular. Marx is not claiming that in the pre-modern world individuals were any the less persons, but that for them individuality and social identity coincided: 'a nobleman always remains a nobleman, a commoner always a commoner, a quality inseparable from his individuality irrespective of his other relations' (1846a: 78). Everybody is somebody's kin, somebody's slave, somebody's client, and these relations establish individuals' very being. Such sociality is internal to personal identity, and subjectivity is experienced as immediately social. Personal dependence is the groundwork of society *and* individual identity. 'Society', accordingly, does not appear as something which is separable from individuals; this appearance is itself an artefact of modernity. When the term 'society' is used at all, in fact, typically (and very revealingly) it refers to the *haute monde*, the personalized networks of the privileged. Capitalism, Marx thinks, changes all this.

'Present-day society', he wrote in 1843, 'is the realised principle of *individualism*; the individual existence is the final goal; activity, work, content, etc., are *mere* means' (1843a: 81). In modern society, he reiterates fifteen years later in the *Grundrisse*, all

> ties of personal dependence, distinctions of birth, education, etc. (all the personal ties at least appear as *personal* relationships), are in fact broken, abolished. The individuals *appear* to be independent ... appear to collide with one another freely, and to exchange with one another in this freedom.
>
> (1858: 100)

Here, personal relations appear – for the first time – *as* 'purely' personal, as distinct from social; an example (not used by Marx himself) might be the 'love marriage', as against the 'arranged marriage' which relates families or lineages through the bonding of individuals. The individual is now conceivable, as a subject, independently of social contexts. Social position concurrently appears as something 'accidental', as 'only an *external* quality of the individual, being neither inherent in his labour nor standing to him in fixed relationships as an objective community organized according to rigid laws' (1843a: 80). It is this solitary individual – 'the individual' in the abstract, without any distinction of, or reference to the 'accidental' particularities of concrete circumstance – who is the moral subject of the modern world. He is sanctified as such in the Rights of Man. I use the masculine universal advisedly. Much of what Marx wrote concerning 'individuals' in *bürgerliche Gesellschaft* openly applied, at least at the time he was writing, only to (some) men. This point, about which I shall say more later, should be kept in mind throughout this chapter.

Marx argues that recognition of this 'juridical person', the abstract subject of the bourgeois order, is implicit in the very activity of commodity exchange. 'The act of exchange', he says, is 'both the positing and the confirmation' not only of exchange values but equally 'of the *subjects* as exchangers'. It is the 'natural' difference of the parties involved – their different products and needs – which motivates exchanges. But in exchange they, like their products, are 'socially equated' as equals. In its form, this is as true of the wage contract as of any other, and Marx sees this appearance as basic to the illusion that wages are an equivalent for work done. Moreover, he argues, since in exchange individuals 'are *presupposed* as and *prove* themselves to be equals, *freedom* comes to play a role in addition to equality'. Like Weber, Marx sees capitalist exchange as (ideally) peaceful. In exchange

> A and B recognize each other as owners, as persons, whose commodities are permeated by their will. Accordingly, the juridical concept of the person comes in here, as well as that of freedom in so far as it is contained therein. Neither forcibly takes possession of the property of the other; each disposes of it voluntarily.

Here 'the individual, each of them, is reflected in himself as the exclusive and dominant (determining) *subject* of the exchange. With that the complete freedom of the individual is posited'. Contrast slavery or serfdom, where for Marx 'appropriation of another's *will*' is exactly what is at issue; the slave is not a subject but a means of production – precisely an object. Unfreedom is of the essence of his or her being. In the *Institutiones* of Justinian, he notes, the *servus* 'is correctly defined as one who can acquire nothing for himself by means of exchange' (1858: 174–7).

Marx argues in various places that 'at first there is *commerce*, and then a *legal order* develops out of it'. As an empirical assertion I think this is dubious. But the key point he is making is that – irrespective of questions of chickens and eggs – 'in a developed trade the exchangers recognize each other tacitly as equal persons ... they *do* this while they offer the goods to one another and agree to trade with one another' (1880: 210). Hence, he argues, 'equality and freedom are not only respected in exchange which is based on exchange values, but the exchange of exchange values is the real productive basis of all *equality* and *freedom*' (1858: 176). Marx generally regarded ideas and categories as but 'abstractions of actual social relations that are transitory and historical' (1846b: 100) – a proposition I think better interpreted through Wittgenstein's idea of meaning residing *in* a 'form of life' (Winch 1958) than through Lenin's metaphor of 'reflection'. The latter suggests the separability of 'matter' and 'spirit', something Marx was at considerable pains to deny (it is fundamental to his critique of the Young Hegelians) (Sayer 1983, 1987).

In this case, he argues, 'as pure ideas, equality and freedom are merely idealized expressions of this exchange; developed in juridical, political and social relations, they are merely this basis to a higher level' (1858: 176). Behind the *citoyen* stands the *bourgeois*. The *'practical* relation' of commodity exchange on the basis of private labour implicitly contains the norms which find their *'legal form'* in the contract (1880: 210). The 'pre-contractual' mores whose indispensability to individual contracts Durkheim (1984) eloquently demonstrated against Spencer are, for Marx, embedded in the form of life that is capitalism. For the 'attributes of the juridical person', he maintains, are 'precisely [those] of the individual engaged in exchange' (1858: Nicolaus ed., 246). The sphere of circulation, as he sardonically put it in *Capital*, is 'a very Eden of the innate rights of man'. There (in contrast to the 'hidden abode' of production, where individuals are classed and subordinated precisely as members of collectivities, 'hands' in the blunter terminology of the nineteenth century) 'alone rule Freedom, Property, Equality and Bentham' (1867a: 176).

Just as the material specificity of use value is effaced in exchange value, so are the differential material circumstances of real individuals ignored in this *fictio juris* who is the ideal subject of *bürgerliche Gesellschaft*. This is crucial, as we shall see, to Marx's analysis of the modern state. It is also paradigmatic, I shall argue, of a great deal more in modernity's representations of subjectivity.

2

But there is another, and a very much darker, side to modern individualism as Marx analyses it. In capitalism *all* social bonds appear external to the individual (and thus, to come back to Baudelaire, ephemeral, fugitive, contingent): 'the various forms of the social nexus confront the individual as merely a means towards his private purposes, as external necessity' (1857: 18). It is this that grounds the appearance of personal freedom – and, I suggest, gives purchase to the means–ends–conditions models of 'action' so beloved of sociology (not to mention 'rational-choice' Marxism). But, Marx argues, although 'individuals seem freer under the dominance of the bourgeoisie than ever before, because their conditions of life seem accidental', 'in reality, of course they are less free, because they are to a greater extent subject to material forces' (1846a: 79). The 'personal limitation of one individual by another' which formed the 'groundwork' of all previous societies is replaced not by substantial freedom, but by the 'objective limitation of the individual by relationships which are independent of him and self-sufficient' (1858: 100–1). Simmel, whose analysis of modern sociality I mentioned above, draws out a phenomenological corollary. He too observes that modernity (and specifically, life in the metropolis) 'secures for the individual a kind and measure of personal freedom for which there exists no analogy' elsewhere. But the 'obverse' of this is that 'one nowhere feels so lonely and lost than in the metropolitan crowd'. Modernity entails 'the atrophy of individual culture through the hypertrophy of objective culture', offering 'such an overpowering wealth of crystallized, impersonalized mind, as it were, that the personality cannot maintain itself when confronted with it'. One (paradoxical) consequence of this may be an 'exaggerated subjectivism'; but, in Marx's terms, this is a subjectivism without objective content (Frisby 1985: 77–86).

Freedom, for Marx, means 'power ... domination over the circumstances and conditions in which an individual lives' (1846a: 301n), and capitalism, from this point of view, represents the apotheosis of *un*freedom. 'Far from abolishing the "relationships of dependence"', capitalism 'dissolve[s] them into a general form' (1858: 101). Personal dependency is replaced by universal dependency. This is the phenomenon Marx analysed in his early writings as alienation, and in *Capital* as fetishism: the estrangement of human products – both material and otherwise – from human beings' control and even recognition. Just as in religion, for Marx, 'the productions of the human brain appear as independent beings endowed with life ... entering into relation both with one another and the human race', 'so it is in the world of commodities with the products of men's hands' (1867a: 72). Like the gods, these estranged products govern human destinies – with the difference that unlike the fictitious deities of religion, this governance is far from merely imaginary. The epitome of such estrangement is 'the market'. In *Capital*, Marx firmly roots this alienation in the social division of labour upon which that market rests.

This division indeed does constitute commodity producers as autonomous subjects, but in a very specific sense. Unlike on the medieval manor or within the 'Asiatic' village community, their activities are not socially regulated. Their labour, both in appearance and in fact, is private. They act independently of one another on the basis of calculations as to returns. But this does not, for Marx, entail any substantial growth in individuals' power over their conditions of life; for most, on the contrary, it diminishes it. For the self-same division of labour engenders 'a whole network of social relations spontaneous in their growth and entirely beyond the control of the actors' (1867a: 112), which proceed to act on them with the coercive force and implacable externality of natural laws (as which, in turn, Political Economy fetishistically misconstrues them):

> The owners of commodities ... find out, that the same division of labour that turns them into independent private producers, also frees the social process of production and the relations of the individual producers to each other within that process, from all dependence on the will of those producers, and the seemingly mutual independence of the individuals is supplemented by a system of general and mutual dependence by means of the products.
>
> (1867a: 107–8)

This is what Marx means when he characterizes modern society as a world of 'personal independence based on dependence *mediated by things*' (1858: 95). Because of the 'purely atomic' character of commodity production, individuals' 'relations to each other ... assume a material character independent of their control and conscious individual action' (1867a: 92–3). This is a world of unintended consequences, in which social relations appear as natural circumstance, not the product of human consciousness or activity.

Within capitalism, people are just as interdependent – as so-cially related – as in any other society; indeed they are more so, in view of both its globality and the extent to which it has divided labour. Anticipating Durkheim's famous paradox of the division of labour rendering individuals both 'more autonomous [...] and yet more linked to society' (1984: xxx), Marx observes that 'the epoch which produces this standpoint, that of the isolated individual, is precisely the epoch of the hitherto most developed social ... relations' (1857: 18). Weber (1970: 139) remarked one ironic con-sequence of this development: inhabitants of modern society have less 'knowledge of the conditions of life under which we live than has an American Indian or a Hottentot' (and knowledge, we should scarcely need Foucault to tell us, is power).

What distinguishes capitalism, for Marx, is the form which this social relatedness takes. Sociality is neither directly and evidently inter-personal, as in his pre-modern world, nor does it take the form – as he hoped it would in communism – of 'the all-round development of the individuals and the subordination of their communal, social productivity' (1858: 95); an appealing, if some-what murky, formulation. In capitalism, to a far greater degree than in the past, 'individuals now only produce for and within so-ciety'. As I outlined in Chapter 1, this becomes the more true, for Marx, the more capitalism progresses: production is increasingly social and exchange increasingly global. But 'their production is not *directly* social, not the offspring of association distributing la-bour within itself. The individuals are subsumed under social pro-duction, which exists outside them as their fate; but social production is not subsumed under the individuals who manage it' (1858: 95–6).

Hence, for Marx, 'the productive forces appear as a world for themselves, quite independent of and divorced from the individ-uals ... whose forces they are' (1846a: 86). It is this alienation of the social, in which human beings' collective capacities manifest themselves as the attributes of material things, which is in his view the ground of modern individualism:

> standing against these productive forces, we have the majority of the individuals from whom these forces have been wrested away, and who, robbed thus of all real life content, have become

abstract individuals, who are, however, by this very fact put in a
position to enter into relation with one another *as individuals*.
(1846a: 87)

People appear to be independent of one another because their
mutual dependency assumes the unrecognizable form of relations
between commodities. The consummation of the 'wresting away'
lies, of course, in the class relation between workers and capitalists. The epitome of the 'abstract individual' is the '*worker*, who is
stripped of all qualities except this one' (1858: 399).

In capitalism, for Marx, individuals thus appear to be self-sufficient monads only because the social relations which really link
them – and give them their concrete identities, for him first and
foremost as members of social classes – do not appear to them as
such, as relations of persons. They assume, on the contrary, 'the
fantastic form of relations between things' (1867a: 72). 'The economy' takes on an existence of its own, quite independently of
anyone's volition. This 'economy' is in fact something which for
the first time actually becomes *conceivable* as an independent domain (and thus as a possible object of a 'science' seeking its 'laws')
only within the modern world, precisely because of this estrangement. In pre-capitalist societies, as we saw, for Marx economic life
was subordinated to social imperatives. Now, 'the economy' is
subject neither to individual nor collective control. It is experienced, rather, as an external environment of action for individuals
– Adam Smith's aptly named 'invisible hand' of 'the market'.

This remains the case, Marx maintains, even when, through laborious scientific analysis, 'its' laws have been comprehended. The
realization that 'the products of labour, in so far as they are values,
are but material expressions of the labour spent on their production ... by no means dissipates the mist through which the social
character of labour appears to us to be an objective character of
the products themselves' (1867a: 74). What Marx terms 'fetishism', the misapprehension of the social as material, is not just a
matter of subjective illusion, but the expression of how things are.
In the transactions of the capitalist economy, individuals' only social connection *is* through the exchange of their products, and it is
solely in the exchange values of these products that their real sociality (as distinct from their ideal subjectivity) is made manifest at

all. It is 'the pressure of general demand and supply upon each other [which] provides the connection between the mutually indifferent individuals' (1858: 95), and 'the relations connecting the labour of one individual, with that of the rest appear, not as direct social relations between individuals at work, but as *what they really are*, material relations between persons and social relations between things' (1867a: 73, my emphasis). Reification is a social process, not a mere category error.

The sovereign individual of capitalism (Abercrombie *et al.* 1986) emerges, then, as a paradoxical creature, whose splendid isolation is the basis for modern society actually becoming, in Émile Durkheim's concept, a reality *sui generis*. Marx would undoubtedly have seen Durkheim's famous proposition as a modern illusion, expressive of exactly the alienation he is analysing; but he would also have recognized that it accurately summates the experience of modern sociality. To echo Tönnies, *bürgerliche Gesellschaft* is no longer a palpable *Gemeinschaft*: and 'society' can appear as 'a single subject', 'an abstraction *vis-à-vis* the individual', an entity 'which accomplishes the mystery of generating itself' (1857: 31; 1844: 299; 1846a: 52), precisely because of this estrangement. The ground of personal freedom – the division of labour – is at the same time the root of an unparalleled objective dependency, in which the very social relations which concretely differentiate people as individuals cease to be recognizable for what they are.

For Marx, this renders bourgeois freedom 'merely imaginary', and bourgeois independence 'merely an illusion' (1858: 100) – though, in his fullest commentary on the topic (1843b), he still sees this as a major advance on the previous '*animal* history of human society' with its explicit differentiation of liberties and privileges on the basis of social standing (1843a: 81). A purely 'political emancipation' is less than fully 'human emancipation', but vastly preferable to no emancipation at all. Unlike some of his followers, Marx did not lightly dismiss human rights. Indeed only their acknowledgement permits him to make the criticisms of *bürgerliche Gesellschaft* that he does. His point was simply that within bourgeois society they remained, for most people, largely chimerical, because they did not extend to that arena which he considered the foundation of all human being, the 'production of life' (1846a: 41) itself. In his view 'only when the real, individual man re-absorbs in himself the abstract citizen, and as an individual human being has become a *species-being* in his everyday life, in his particular work, and in his particular situation ... and consequently no longer separates social power from himself in the shape of *political* power, only then will human emancipation be accomplished' (1843b: 168). The 'abstract individual' who is claimed to enjoy political and civil rights is just that: a representation, a subject whose existence is merely ideal (in all senses of the word). But it is this subject – free, equal and independent – who is the universal reference point for all bourgeois political, legal and ethical discourses, and the novel technologies of moral regulation they articulate.

3

In capitalism, then, in contrast to all former societies, 'there appears a cleavage in the life of each individual, in so far as it is personal and in so far as it is determined by some branch of labour and the conditions pertaining to it' (1846a: 78). Formerly these coincided, Marx thinks. Both the notion of 'the personal' as pertaining purely to the individual, and the allied conception of social position as 'accidental' – a 'role', as the sociologists have it – as something extrinsic to the individual, are for him new. This has important implications for the forms in which social power is exercised. It no longer works through relationships of personal domination and servitude, nor is it inscribed in the unitary identity of the individual, as lord or serf, *dominus* and *servus*. Like everything else in the bourgeois world, social power too is 'mediated by things'. If in the pre-capitalist era power over persons was the basis for power over their products – if 'the *relationship of domination*', in Marx's words, was 'an essential relation of appropriation' (1858: 424) – then in capitalism it is the other way about.

The 'things' in question, for Marx, are those which are, or are capable of becoming, capital – exchange values and money. This follows directly from the alienation discussed above. In a society where social relations take the form of relations between things, one must command those things in order to command people.

'The power that each individual exercises over the activity of others or over social wealth exists in him', Marx says, 'as the owner of *exchange values*, of *money*. He carries his social power, as also his connection with society, in his pocket' (1858: 94). Power is externalized, residing now in objective forms outside of people rather than in their differential subjective identities. It is, literally, disembodied. And it is this objectification which enables power to be exercised by individuals *as* individuals rather than as personifications of a community. It is no longer inscribed in their particular social personalities but instead becomes a *thing* which can be privately *possessed*, in principle by anyone. Its essential character as a relationship of persons is obscured by the 'material' forms through which it is mediated.

Money – the 'social résumé' of the world of commodities – is for Marx 'something general in which all individuality, all particularity, is negated and extinguished' (1858: 94). It is 'a commodity, an external object, capable of becoming the private property of any individual' (1867a: 132). Its acquisition confers social power independently of birth, rank and status: and 'this relationship to a thing quite unconnected with [its possessor's] individuality gives him at the same time [...] general domination over society, over the whole world of enjoyment, labour, etc' – including, above all, the possibility of using it to employ others and command their surplus labour, in ever more abstracted and impersonal ways (consider the workings of the stock market). Money, Marx says, is the social equivalent of the philosopher's stone (1858: 154–5). In it, 'social power becomes the private power of private persons', and like almost everything else in capitalism it escapes any social control. For that reason, he observes, it was roundly denounced by the ancients as 'subversive of the economic and moral order of things' (1867a: 132).

Marx posits a stark alternative, which serves as well as any other criterion to divide 'past' and 'present' as he sees them:

> In exchange value, the social attitude of persons is transformed into a social attitude of things; personal capacity into a capacity of things. The less social power the means of exchange possesses, the more closely it is still connected with the nature of the immediate product of labour and the immediate needs of its

exchangers, the greater must that power of the community still be which binds together the individuals, the patriarchal relationship, the community of antiquity, feudalism and the guild system.

Every individual possesses social power in the form of a thing. Take away this social power from the thing, and you must give it to persons [to exercise] over persons.

(1858: 94–5)

It is exactly, and only, this possession of social power in the form of 'things' – commodities, money, capital – which defines the modern bourgeoisie, in relation to one another, in relation to propertyless labour, *and* by contrast to former ruling classes, whose power assumed different forms altogether. Two important points follow from this.

The first I have touched on above. It is in capitalism, according to Marx for the first time in history, that social power – and the exploitation through which it is reproduced – take on a 'purely economic' form. The subjection of the modern labourer to capital, he argues (I think, overstating the case), is guaranteed by 'the dull compulsion of economic relations'; 'direct force, outside economic conditions, is of course still used, but only exceptionally. In the ordinary run of things, the labourer can be left to the "natural laws of production"' (1867a: 737). In pre-capitalist societies, this was not so. The mechanisms of exploitation were 'extra-economic', and rested on personalized dependence (1865a: 790–2). Violence, or its threat, was an essential element in such relations, whether the power of life and death over wife, children and slaves held by the ancient Roman *paterfamilias*, or the jurisdiction which the medieval lord enjoyed over his tenants and serfs; Anthony Giddens (1981) has recently underlined the modernity of the wage relation in this respect. Corresponding to this removal of physical violence (including its juridical forms) from the sphere of what are now regarded as 'private' relations, for Marx as much as for Weber, is the monopolization of the legitimate use of force in the hands of the modern state. I shall come back to the latter in a minute. It should be emphasized, however, that Marx is speaking specifically here of class; whether all power relations (gender, 'race') in 'modern' society fit this model is highly debatable.

My second point, however, is the more contentious. This is, quite simply, that class is *itself* a modern category. Class is a different kind of social relationship than its equivalents in the pre-capitalist world. I do not mean by this that surplus labour and exploitation were the invention of capitalism. Nor do I deny that Marx himself used the term class to describe various pre-capitalist social groupings. As Maurice Godelier (1984) has noted, there are two usages of the word in Marx's writings, a broad one (any relation involving the appropriation of surplus labour) and one that is historically specific. It is the latter I am concerned with here. Marx was insistent that the first such social group in history to rule *as* a class was the bourgeoisie. 'The difference between the private individual and the class individual, the accidental nature of the conditions of life for the individual', he maintains, 'appears *only* with the emergence of the class, *which is itself a product of the bourgeoisie*' (1846a: 78, my emphasis). Class, here, is distinct from estate (in the German, *Stand*), and this distinction is a critical one in Marx's theorization of what is so new about the modern world.

Bourgeois power and proletarian powerlessness are founded in relations to property, in the modern sense outlined above. What makes class different from estate – or from any previous form of social distinction – is *that* it appears as a 'purely economic' relation. But the very existence of 'pure' property relations is contingent upon capitalism's 'emancipation of private property from the community' (1846a: 79), its severing of property from its 'former social and political embellishments and associations' (1865a: 618). This is not to deny that this 'economic' relation may provide the basis for the development of differential identities and cultural forms, marked by everything from meal times to accent, or that other social differences, for instance of 'race' or gender, may in practice determine who falls into which 'economic' class. But class appears to be less internal or essential a component of subjectivity than is caste, or servility, or slavery – in sum, those relations Max Weber analysed in terms of 'status'. It presents itself as a matter of mere 'accidental' circumstance rather than inherent being, as something which is extrinsic to the essence of personality.

The point is not merely that – as Marx recognizes – capitalism offers more individual mobility than previous forms of society. It is rather that class does not seem to define the individual in the same way. There *is* an apparent split between the 'private individual' and the 'class individual', which is predicated upon the 'accidental' nature of that which makes individuals members of classes – their property in 'things' external to themselves. In principle anybody may own property, just as all are free to stay at the Ritz Hotel. This is not the case for, say, caste, or nobility, or – within slave and serf societies – freeborn status. Nor is it, I would again stress, true of all marks of social difference in the 'modern' world.

Marx argues that this division between the 'private' and the 'class' individual exists within, and compromises the sense of collective identity of, both the bourgeoisie and the proletariat. 'Competition separates individuals from one another, not only the bourgeois but still more the workers, in spite of the fact that it brings them together' (1846a: 75). There is, as the famous uncompleted closing chapter of *Capital* 3 (a mere 40 lines entitled 'Classes') puts it, an 'infinite fragmentation of interest and rank into which the division of social labour splits labourers as well as capitalists and landlords' (1865a: 886). Hence, 'every organized power standing over against these isolated individuals, who live in conditions daily reproducing this isolation, can only be overcome after long struggles' (1846a: 75). As for the bourgeoisie, 'the separate individuals form a class only in so far as they have to carry on a battle against another class; in other respects they are on hostile terms with each other as competitors' (1846a: 77). *Capital* puts this in Hobbesian terms: 'the division of labour within the society brings into contact independent commodity-producers, who acknowledge no other authority but that of competition, of the coercion exerted by the pressure of their mutual interests; just as in the animal kingdom, the *bellum omnium contra omnes* more or less preserves the conditions of existence of every species' (1867a: 356). C. B. Macpherson has of course argued that behind Hobbes's war of all against all stands emergent capitalism; it was seventeenth-century England's nascent 'market society' that provided the paradigm for the 'state of nature' which brought forth his Leviathan (1962).

In this, specifically modern sense of the term, Peter Laslett

(1973) might have been quite correct to characterize pre-industrial England as a 'one-class society', and E. P. Thompson equally insightful when he argued that there is a sense in which class struggle precedes class (1978), which is, as he put it, not a thing but a 'happening' (1965: 85; cf. his 1968 Introduction): a form of communality which is not simply given but is made in and through social struggles. Unlike an estate, a class is something which can be conceived of as existing 'in itself', within a network of 'objective' (that is to say, of alienated) property relations, but by no means necessarily 'for itself', as a self-conscious social grouping. This distinction, a celebrated one in Marx (see his 1852: 187–8), would have made very little sense in his pre-capitalist world. It is itself modern. A consciousness of class membership and identification of oneself by class membership are not an integral dimension *of* class membership, because sociality has been alienated in things and divorced from personal identity. Capitalism, in short, renders those forms of social relationship which materially give to individuals their concrete and particular identities – which meant, so far as Marx was concerned, above all else their class positions – peculiarly external (and therefore by no means transparent) to them.

One implication of this is obvious. If, as Marx argues, consciousness is founded in social being, then undermining the possibility of class consciousness – on both sides – is the individualizing division of labour which is as constitutive a relation of capitalism as class itself. The modern world is an atomistic, fissiparous kind of place, and social identities are abidingly fragmented and contradictory. The subject is unified in terms of *personal* biography, but dislocated from any *social* integument; and these go hand in hand to produce a thoroughly idealized representation of 'the individual'. Émile Durkheim's 'anomie' and 'egoism', and the experience of class disadvantage as personal inadequacy, would therefore seem as structurally inherent in capitalism as any new forms of solidarity (which is not to deny that the latter are *possible*). So would the intra-class conflicts on the basis of market opportunities emphasized by Max Weber: for in the market-place labour appears as but another more or less scarce resource, exactly equivalent to capital, a mere 'factor of production'. Notwithstanding the socialization of production and polarization of classes discussed above, then, capitalism produces, and endlessly reproduces, the isolated, abstract, *individuals*, their social relations apparent to them only in alienated and mystified forms, who are implicit in its divisions of labour. What Marx saw as capitalism's most basic contradiction, between its increasingly social productive forces and its enduringly privatized mode of appropriation, reaches deep: into our selves. Modernity constitutes individuals as subjects not through but in opposition to the real sociality which concretely defines and differentiates them.

4

If class, in this sense, is a modern phenomenon, then so is the state, the final social form I wish to examine in this chapter. Once again, this is not to deny that forms of 'public' governance and authority existed prior to capitalism, nor even that they were ordinarily controlled by ruling 'classes' (in Marx's wider sense of that term). The question is again one of forms. And here Marx is categorical:

> The political constitution as such is brought into being only where the private spheres have won an independent existence. Where trade and landed property are not free and have not yet become independent, the political constitution too does not yet exist.... The abstraction of the *state as such* belongs only to modern times, because the abstraction of private life belongs only to modern times. The abstraction of the *political state* is a modern product.
>
> (1843a: 31–2)

It is, he argues, through 'the emancipation of private property from the community' that 'the state has become a separate entity, beside and outside civil society' (1846a: 79). 'The *establishment of the political state* and the dissolution of civil society into independent *individuals* ... is accomplished by *one and the same act*' (1843b: 167). This should perhaps not be taken literally, in that historically state formation long preceded capitalism, most notably in its English 'classic ground', and probably was, as theorists from Weber to Braudel have argued, a *sine qua non* for capitalist development (Corrigan and Sayer 1985). Marx himself acknowledged (à propos England) that 'governments ... appear as conditions of the historic dissolution process and as makers of the conditions of existence of capital' (1858: 431). The key point, however, is that irrespective of the historical origins of either, for him capitalism entails 'the abstraction of the political state'. As he expressed it in *The German Ideology*, *bürgerliche Gesellschaft* 'must assert itself in its external relations as nationality and internally must organize itself as state' (1846a: 89).

Notwithstanding its democratic and universalistic claims, Marx argues that the modern state is in substance as much a form in which the holders of social power secure their domination as any pre-capitalist mode of rule. It is, for him, 'the ruling class', the bourgeoisie, which 'constitutes its joint domination as public power, as the state' (1846a: 355). It does so in a peculiar way. The state, Marx suggests, is oddly marginal and central within bourgeois society at the same time, in that its major activity is to secure the conditions under which the bourgeoisie can operate privately *as* individuals, in 'civil society'. It appears less intrusive than its pre-capitalist counterparts, even if freedom of the market, as Adam Smith (quoted in Winch 1978: 88–9) put it, ever depends on 'the orderly oppression of law'. This market freedom, I would argue, also rests upon a much more comprehensive moral regulation of social relations and identities, through a plethora of agencies for the re-formation of character (Corrigan and Sayer 1985; Corrigan 1990) – a dimension of modernity on which, as we shall see, Max Weber has much to say. The author of *The Theory of Moral Sentiments* would not have disagreed. There is nothing unusual in those who possess social power also wielding 'political' power. What is novel is this form which bourgeois rule takes. It is the organization of this social power in the shape of a 'political' state, ostensibly independent of civil society and its 'private' power relations – those based in the ownership of property – which is, for Marx, so uniquely modern. The rule of a *class* and the *form* of the 'political state' (as distinct from earlier modes of governance) are for him internally related (Ollman 1976).

It is because, he argues, the bourgeoisie is a class – not an estate – a congeries of otherwise divided individuals, that their personal rule must at the same time assume the form of average rule. Their personal power is based on conditions of life which as they develop are common to many individuals, and the continuance of which they, as ruling individuals, have to maintain against others and, at the same time, to maintain that they hold good for everybody.

(1846a: 329)

Since the bourgeoisie does not rule through personalized relations, public power must assume impersonal forms. Marx sees both the 'rule of law' (for Weber equally an essential condition of modern capitalism) and representative democracy as expressions of this exigency. Both presume a civil society of abstractly equal free individuals. 'It is precisely because the bourgeoisie rules as a class', he says, 'that in the law it must give itself a general expression', an expression that is 'independent of the personal arbitrariness of each individual among them'. It is

because individuals who are independent of one another assert themselves and their own will, and because on this basis their attitude to one another is bound to be egoistical, that self-denial is made necessary in law and right, self-denial in the exceptional case, and self-assertion of their interests in the average case.

(1846a: 329)

Universalistic, rational, consistent law provides a level playing field. This contrasts starkly with the explicitly differential 'privileges' of medieval society, where noblemen, for instance, were exempt from corporal punishment and the first estate enjoyed 'benefit of clergy', that is, immunity from prosecution in public courts. The latter was also, for the most part, an exclusively masculine prerogative.

Similarly with democracy. 'The representative system', Marx writes, 'is a very specific product of modern bourgeois society which is as inseparable from the latter as is the isolated individual of modern times'. It is the appropriate form for the 'political rule of the bourgeois *class*' – a class of equal individuals, within a society of formally equal individuals – in contrast to the hierarchized 'ruling *estates*' of the medieval world (1846a: 200). Again the modernity of such a conception of society, as that community which claims to embrace all (and therefore, in its official representation as state, claims the lives and the loyalties of all) is worth underlining. Marx also anticipated recent writers in playing on the double meaning of 'representation'. As the state, he argues, 'the nation attains existence as a *notion*, a fantasy, an illusion, a *representation* – as the *represented* nation ... cut off from the real nation' (1843a: 69–70).

Fundamental to the modern state form is a clear separation of 'public' and 'private', and the basis of this separation is that 'cleavage in the life of the individual' we have already examined. It is as an abstract individual, a free and equal legal person, independently of the 'accidents' of 'circumstance' that one is a subject of the modern state. Again Marx develops his argument through contrasts with pre-capitalist societies, notably feudalism. In medieval society, he argues, in what we would nowadays consider to be the 'political' sphere (but the very term is anachronistic) there simply was no distinction of 'public' and 'private'. The social statuses which gave to individuals their 'civil' identities also directly conferred or excluded them from 'political' power. *'Feudalism ... was directly political*, that is to say, the elements of civil life, for example, property, or the family, or the mode of labour, were raised to the level of political life in the form of seignory, estates, and corporations.' Subjectivities were correspondingly differentiated. Consistently with this, 'the unity of the state' appeared as 'the *particular* affair of a ruler isolated from the people, and of his servants' (1843b: 165–6). To govern was seen as a natural attribute (and often represented as a divine right) of definite, socially located individuals.

Such rulers, from the king down to the humblest lord of the manor, did not partition their 'public' and 'private' selves. Monarchs 'lived off their own', taxes were farmed, noble birth conferred the right and duty to sit in parliaments, and so on. The same is true of the 'aristocratic civism' of antiquity. Graeco-Roman 'evergetism', as Paul Veyne (1987) calls it, whereby notables met the costs of endowing their cities with lavish monuments and provided the plebeians with bread and circuses out of their own pockets expresses a similar ethos. One consequence of this unity of

'public' and 'private' is what some historians of medieval feudalism have referred to as the 'parcellization of sovereignty' – its dis-
persal throughout the multiple personal relations which made up
'society' (if that term has any purchase at all in this context). Another way of putting this would be to say that the very idea of
sovereignty is a modern one which would have made little sense in
the feudal world, except, perhaps, as an attribute of divinity, the
only 'all-embracing unity' (Marx 1858: 400) that was conceivable
under such conditions of pervasive and acknowledged social differentiation. Thomas Hobbes, who knew what he was about,
called the state 'Mortall God', thereby sacrilegiously marking an
epochal transformation. Both Marx and Durkheim were to employ similar imagery.

The modern state doubly fractures this coincidence of the 'public' and the 'private'. Sovereignty is consolidated in an apparently
impersonal apparatus – 'the state' which, like 'the economy', its
conjoined twin, we can also only properly begin to conceptualize
as an independent domain (and in this case make the object of
'political science') in 'modern times'. Jurisdiction, administration
and (by no means least) the right to use force are centralized. As
Marx put it, speaking of modern France (and writing in idiosyn-
cratic English), 'the seigneurial privileges of the medieval lords
and cities and clergy were transformed into the attributes of a unitary state power, displacing the feudal dignitaries by salaried state
functionaries, transferring the arms from medieval retainers of
the landlords and corporations of townish citizens to a standing
army, substituting for the checkered (party coloured) anarchy of
conflicting medieval powers the regulated plan of a state power,
with a systematic and hierarchic division of labour' (1871: 483–4).
Along with this goes a cultural revolution of equal profundity.
The nation state itself becomes the embodiment of 'society', and
the new basis of individuals' public identities. The erstwhile 'Earl
of Derby's man' (and member of the community of Christendom,
equal with all only in Thomas Aquinas's *communitas divina*) is
now, first and foremost, a subject – in the other sense of the term
– of the English Crown, a *national* citizen. Weber was to address
this facet of state formation and its connection with capitalism
more fully than Marx, dubbing the bourgeoisie, in a brief phrase

which encapsulates so much, the 'national citizen class' (1966: 249). But Marx did register the profound transformations of social identity involved.

Previously, an individual's social position had 'secluded the individual from the state as a whole and ... converted the *particular* relation of his corporation to the state as a whole into his general relation to the life of the nation' (1843b: 166). It would be more accurate to say the individual had no relation either to 'the state as a whole' or to 'the life of the nation', since neither of these could be said to exist in their modern meanings. Individuals derived their identities, at once 'private' and 'public', from the particularities of their social positions, period. The apocryphal story of the Emperor Charles V, who supposedly said he spoke Spanish to God, Italian to women, French to men and German to his horse, illustrates this nicely (and in a critical arena of state formation, language). But with the rise of the modern state, Marx argues, 'a person's *distinct* activity and distinct situation in life were reduced to a *merely individual* significance', and 'public affairs as such ... became the general affair of each individual, and the political function became the individual's general function' (ibid.). It is the abstraction of individuality which is the ground of citizenship, the form of membership in a community which is characteristic of and specific to the modern world. Ideas of citizenship did, of course, exist long before capitalism, but within the ancient and medieval world they were indices of difference, allowing St Paul, for example, to escape a whipping because he had the privileged status of *civis Romanus*. Modernity, in extending the notion to all, changes its meaning. It is precisely differences that are abstracted from. 'This *man*, the member of civil society', Marx concludes, 'is ... the basis, the precondition, of the *political* state' (ibid.).

Implicit in all this is a separation of the institutions of ruling from the persons of rulers whose most general expression, for Marx as for Weber, lies in bureaucracy. Like money, political power also becomes a 'thing', which we can think of as capable of being 'captured', 'shared' or 'smashed'. Feudal bonds of fealty and homage, because of their intrinsically personalized nature, could never be represented thus. Weber too draws this contrast with the 'pre-modern' world, as we shall see. Political power is incarnated in an apparatus rather than being embodied in persons (the conception of a 'body politic', originally a metaphorical extension of the body of the King, provides a bridge from the one to the other). It is abstracted from individual subjectivities and enshrined in an objective 'machine'. The norms of earlier governance – tax farming, evergetism and the like – would be viewed, in this modern world, as corruption: the systematic and morally unacceptable 'confusion' of private and public interests. Marx maintains that bureaucracy is 'based on *this separation*' between 'particular interests' (those of the individuals of civil society) and what is 'intrinsically and explicitly general' (1843a: 45). It is simply 'the other side' (1843a: 117) of the division of the person between the private individual and the public citizen, the 'imaginary state alongside the real state' (1843a: 47), which purports to embody the 'general will'.

Bureaucracy, as analysed by Marx, has some quite remarkably Weberian (and indeed some very Foucauldian) characteristics. It is distinguished by a systematic division of labour and a clear hierarchy of authority. Like Weber, Marx employs the analogy of the machine: the principles of bureaucracy are those of 'passive obedience, of faith in authority, of the *mechanism* of fixed and formalistic behaviour'. Bureaucratic hierarchy, he says, 'is a *hierarchy of knowledge*. The top entrusts the understanding of detail to the lower levels, whilst the lower levels credit the top with understanding of the general' ('and so', he sourly adds, 'all are mutually deceived'). '*Authority* is the basis of its knowledge', and the claim to knowledge the basis of its authority (1843a: 46–7). In a prescient article of 1843, which occasioned the closing down by the Prussian government of his newspaper the *Rheinische Zeitung*, Marx scathingly dissected 'the contradiction between the real nature of the world and that ascribed to it in government offices', concluding that 'even the most patent reality appears illusory compared with the reality depicted in the dossiers, which is official' (1843c: 343–4). Because the bureaucracy is held to embody the nation, any challenges to its construction of reality will appear as *merely* private: at best sectional, at worse treasonal (1843a: 47), but always lacking in authority because unauthorized by power. 'The general spirit of the bureaucracy is the *secret*, the mystery, preserved within itself by the hierarchy and against the outside world by being a closed corporation' (ibid.).

Symptomatic of this is the use of examinations – the demonstration of 'technical' accreditation – as the method of entry into state service: this '"link" between the "office of State" and the "individual"', says Marx, 'is nothing but the *bureaucratic baptism of knowledge*, the official recognition of the *transsubstantiation* of profane into sacred knowledge (in every examination, it goes without saying, the examiner knows all)' (1843a: 51). By such means 'administration and political governing' become

> mysteries, transcendent functions only to be trusted to the hands of a trained caste, state parasites, richly paid sycophants and parasites, in the higher posts, absorbing the intelligences of the masses and turning them against themselves in the lower places in the hierarchy.
>
> (1871: 488)

State servants are salaried, and 'in the case of the individual bureaucrat, the state objective turns into his private objective, a *chasing after higher posts*, the *making of a career*' (1843a: 47). Finally, and again as for Weber, bureaucracy has a dialectic of its own in which means usurp ends. As Marx puts it, 'the bureaucracy takes itself to be the ultimate purpose of the state', 'turns its "formal" objectives into its content [and] comes into conflict everywhere with "real" objectives. It is therefore obliged to pass off the form for the content and the content for the form' (1843a: 46).

In the bureaucracy, civil reality is paralleled (not to say parodied) by official reality, or 'the "illusion of the state"', which, Marx says, 'exist[s] as various fixed bureaucratic minds, bound together in subordination and passive obedience' (1843a: 47). Like Durkheim – whose observations on the modern state have been scandalously neglected by sociologists determined to enlist his work for the conservative cause – Marx remarks the sanctification of this 'Holy State Power' (1871: 488) as the totem of the 'nation' which it claims to represent (and actually does much to construct). Durkheim considered the 'concerting' of *représentations collectives* to be the *raison d'être* of the state. The latter was for him 'the very organ of social thought', and 'supremely the organ of moral discipline' – a far more telling conception of the nature of state power, in my view, than Lenin's 'bodies of armed men, prisons, etc.' (Durkheim 1957: 49–50, 72). It also alerts us to the moral and symbolic dimension of what Weber (1978a: Part 1, Chapter 3) was to identify as the *legitimate* monopoly of force as well. Prisons contain those without as well as those within, materializing a moral message. Like armies – armies, in the modern world, not of princes and their retainers (or mercenaries), but of nations and their citizens – prisons are collective representations, symbols of a (claimed) communal identity and ethic of which the individual citizen (compulsorily) partakes.

It was Durkheim (1984), of course, who among sociologists first argued the salience of crime for the construction of 'social solidarity'; thus is normality defined. Marx likewise noted this 'concerting' of communality on the part of the state, arguing that within bourgeois society 'all common institutions are set up with the help of the state and are given a political form' (1846a: 90). Durkheim, here foreshadowing Foucault, also remarked on the connection between modern forms of power and subjectivity which I have argued is central to Marx's account: 'it is only through the state', he claimed, 'that individualism is possible' (1957: 64). The individualism in question is not egoism but a specifically *moral* individualism, entailing a sacralization of 'the human person' as such. 'This is a religion in which man is at once the worshipper and the god' (Durkheim 1973: 46), and its holy of holies is precisely Marx's modern subject, 'Man' in the abstract. Durkheim's commentaries on this novel divinity are among the most insightful sociology has produced. Blasphemy it may be, but such humanism is in his terms (1976) religious, not secular.

The formal separation of public power from civil life gives ground for the appearance of the independence of the state. In terms of personnel, there may indeed be real independence, since unlike former rulers the bourgeoisie do not wield power in their persons. State servants are career bureaucrats, politicians are elected officials. Marx argues of Napoleon III's 1851 *coup d'état* that the French state had 'grown so independent of society itself that a grotesquely mediocre adventurer with a hungry band of desperadoes behind him sufficed to wield it' (1871: 485), whilst insisting that the Second Empire remained in substance a form of bourgeois rule. He also – in my view quite wrongly – saw nineteenth-century Britain as a society in which the bourgeoisie ruled, whilst the 'aristocracy' governed (1855a). It is not at all far-fetched to see grounds here for regarding 'party', as did Weber (1978a: 284–8, 938) as a major dimension of power in modern society which is irreducible to class or status, although Marx would himself have contended that it cannot transcend the deeper realities of class relations, for – in his view – the ultimate source of social power within capitalist society remains the ownership of things. The very existence of the 'political' state is for him a corollary of this alienation: the premiss upon which this social form rests is the same division of labour which grounds capitalist economy itself.

In the state, Marx suggests, we have a transformation of community which exactly complements – and is grounded in – the transformation of individuality discussed earlier. The state is 'the ideal community', in which 'the whole civil society of an epoch is epitomized' (1846a: 90). Eric Wolf (1987) has recently argued that it is the boundaries of the nation state which today delineate our conceptions of 'society' itself. Those things which we take to be definitive of 'a society' (like a 'shared' language, culture and territory) have been *made* such through state formation and the representations of collectivity and subjectivity that it entails. There is scope here for a rich sociology of those ways in which signifiers of identity like language and ethnicity are mobilized in state-making, and Marx himself barely scratched the surface. Undoubtedly nationality and nationalism (and, more broadly, the importance of political ideologies as such) – phenomena of the modern world which are impossible, in the late twentieth century, to ignore – are major lacunae in his sociology, even if he gave some pointers as to their connection with the modern state form. The fundamental mistakenness of the *Manifesto*'s contention that 'the working men have no country ... national differences and antagonisms between peoples are daily more and more vanishing' (1848: 502–3) was to be tragically demonstrated, not for the first or the last time, in the collapse of the Second International following the outbreak of war in 1914. Today, in the wake of the downfall of communist regimes across Europe, the same differences and antagonisms are resurfacing, immune, it seems, to decades of 'internationalist' rhetoric. Marx, I think, greatly underestimated (or failed to anticipate) the specifically *cultural* power of the modern state, a power which derives from the plausibility of its claim to represent essential components of *individual* identities, to epitomize who we are (Corrigan and Sayer 1985).

But he was very clear on one point. Anticipating Benedict Anderson (1983), he contends that the modern nation state is a wholly *imagined* community; once more, an abstraction. Everything in it has 'a double meaning, a real and a bureaucratic meaning' (1843a: 47). The *Grundrisse* contrasts 'natural membership of a community', as found in the pre-capitalist forms discussed earlier, with 'the abstraction of a community whose members have nothing in common but language etc., and barely even that'. The second, Marx maintains, 'is plainly the product of much later historical circumstances' (1858: 414). In the former, there is no disjunction of individuality and communality, and what makes people individuals *is* their membership of the commune. This may very well constitute them differentially, in ways whose explicit acknowledgement (as Weber was later to spell out) is basic to forms of rule and their legitimation. There is, however, nothing imagined or ideological about such an identity. In the 'ideal community' of the modern state, matters are reversed. The differences which concretely give to individuals their real identities – their positions and relations in 'civil society' – are effaced. These relations assume the alien guise of relations between things, appearing as 'circumstance', 'accident', 'the economy': entirely personal concerns, incidental to communality. But as a *citoyen*, a subject of the political state, the individual 'must step out of his civil reality, disregard it, and withdraw from this whole organization into his individuality'. 'The sole existence which he finds for his citizenship of the state is his sheer, blank, *individuality*', a subjectivity without social content (1843a: 77). This subjectivity is the void filled by representations of sociality which relocate the individual in an imagined landscape of fictitious communalities and invented traditions, and the state is both the orchestrator and the site of these representations. A striking recent demonstration of this is to be found in a seminal article in which Peter Linebaugh and Marcus

Rediker show the comprehensive dismemberment, within histories framed by 'nation' and 'race', of the political agency of what was, in the eighteenth century, a multi-'racial' *Atlantic* proletariat (1990). This violence of abstraction, they argue, is founded in violence of another sort; the task of an emancipatory historiography is literally to re-member it.

Thus, for Marx, '*political* man is only abstract, artificial man, man as an *allegorical, juridical* person' (1843b: 167); a subjectivity which is not the individual's 'own, actual, empirical existence', but that of '*quite another being*, a *different*, distinct, opposed being' (1843a: 78). This juridical person is, in a striking phrase, 'the imaginary member of an illusory sovereignty ... deprived of his real individual life and endowed with an unreal universality' (1843b: 154). Nowadays it has become common to talk of the ideological project of the state. Marx's point is that in fundamental ways 'the state' *is* an ideological project, whose ideal transcendence of the real differences of 'civil society' is as illusory as is religion's transcendence of the mundane world. He persistently draws the analogy: 'the relation of the political state to civil society', he maintains, 'is as spiritual as the relation of heaven to earth' (ibid.). The idea of the state is what Philip Abrams (1988; cf. Denis 1989), playing on Durkheim, called a collective *mis*representation of bourgeois society, whose real content remains the inequities of capitalism. It is indeed Mortall God, Aquinas's *communitas Dei* secularized. In fine, then, the same alienation that makes individuals' concrete social relations appear to them as a world of things, 'the economy', grounds an equally abstract representation of their communality, 'the state'. Sinewing the two is the imagined subject of the modern world order, Marx's '"pure" individual ... of the ideologists' (1846a: 78).

5

Let me interject an observation of my own here, which is related to capitalism's coexistence with (and often, historically, its dependence upon) a range of social relations other than those directly involved in the production and exchange of commodities, to which I drew attention in Chapter 1. I suggested there that not all in the modern world is 'modern', or to put it differently capitalism may generalize (or at least allow room for) apparently 'traditional' relations which in turn become premisses of its own existence. My examples were supposedly 'pre-capitalist' labour regimes (like American slavery) and family forms. This, I think, requires us to qualify Marx's analysis of the relation between the modern subject and the political state, along similar lines. He was in any case, in the texts drawn upon immediately above, criticizing radical democratic aspirations rather than analysing any actual state. His 'political state' is best treated as an ideal-type whose 'pure' realization is rare, and historically contingent; though as a paradigm of representation it is, I would argue, of undoubted centrality to the understanding of modernity. It may be that Marx is describing an inherent tendency of modern society, inasmuch as once equality is proclaimed people tend to demand it. But if so, this should not blind us to what have thus far been the plain facts of the matter.

The 'political' citizenship Marx discusses (and the 'civil' rights which go with it) have *never* extended to all individuals who live within civil societies. Various categories of persons, which include those without real property, women, children, the 'insane', prisoners, migrant workers, members of unacceptable faiths, and those with different colour skins, have variously been excluded from the 'ideal community', or admitted to it only in an explicitly subordinated status. These exclusions, in turn, have been fundamental to the ways in which that community has been imagined. Illuminating as it may be, Marx's focus on the abstraction of the individual as the basis for civic citizenship therefore needs to be complemented by an awareness of the degree to which, *within* the 'ideal community' thus constructed, state agencies and actions regulate what, for civic purposes, is to count as a *bona fide* 'individual'. The raising of 'property, family, and the mode of labour' to become 'elements of political life' by no means died out with the Middle Ages. Here, once again, the clearest, though far from the only, example – both of moral regulation of differences, and of Marx's blindness to it – is gender. Regulation here does not only extend to establishing qualifications for the franchise. Equally important is that more pervasive 'concerting' of *représentations col-*

lectives noted by Émile Durkheim, upon which the plausibility of such qualification itself depends.

In his discussion in *Capital* of the nineteenth-century English Factory Acts (1867a: Chapter 10) Marx does not comment upon the social classifications they establish. The 'labour force' (a category which already reduces work to waged labour) is divided between: (1) Adult Males, (2) Women and Young Persons, (3) Children. This is not unconnected (both as cause and effect) with the definition of citizenship. In England in 1867 women did not have the vote, and when, more than half a century later, they were 'granted' it, the age qualification was higher than for males. Nor did four out of five Englishmen or – to register another pervasive dimension of such state-regulated difference – 19 out of 20 Irishmen. In Canada, women first gained the legal status of 'persons' in 1929 (by Order of the British Privy Council!). Within the 'civil' sphere, in England (married) women did not have the same rights to own property or enter into contracts as men until 1935. In the home of bourgeois democracy, much admired as such by Marx, the United States of America, the Equal Rights Amendment failed to pass Congress in 1983 – the centennial of Marx's death. In Britain and North America, the patriarchal family has for long provided a powerful and a pivotal metaphor of state, underpinning and legitimating definitions of the nature of the community and the meaning of full civic individuality within it.

Marx's 'abstract individual', in short, has long carried with *him* a train of *personal dependants*, and this supposedly pre-modern relation has been constitutive of his – and their – subjectivities. As Foucault (1982) has observed, states empower, in ways that are both concrete and differential, as well as oppress. 'The subject' is gendered (not to mention aged, classed and raced). This in turn may be part of the reason why Marx's imagined national community has proven to be far more durable than he expected. 'The state' is a tapestry woven of the most basic strands of social relationship and personal identity – which is also to say, of social differences organized into powers of individuals (Corrigan 1990).

The abstract equality of capitalism's polity, then, need embrace only those who are deemed 'independent' and therefore capable of making voluntary contracts, exactly as in Justinian's *Institutes*; that is, those who are able to acquire something for themselves by means of exchange. Marx's equation of the citizen with the bourgeois – the commodity exchanger – has sometimes held quite literally. The state, at least in the English case, was in place as a form of bourgeois social power long before *les autres* were admitted, slowly and carefully, into the 'society' it claimed to represent (Corrigan and Sayer 1985, Chapter 6). Bourgeois political theory was at one time refreshingly clear on this. For John Locke, for example, only the (male) propertied 'have a full interest in the preservation of property, and only they are capable of that rational life – that voluntary obligation to the law of reason – which is the necessary basis of full participation in civil society'. This equation of property and rationality was common ground at the time he was writing, and for long after. Hence, he concluded, 'civil society was to be in control of the men of property', while the rest ('the greatest part of mankind') became 'an object of state policy, an object of administration, rather than fully a part of the citizen body' (cited in Macpherson 1962: 248, 256, 224).

For those (and they have often been the majority) whose place in this 'society' is to be administered and policed as objects, subjectivity is more problematic even than Marx allows, and the gulf between concrete circumstance and its abstract representation still greater. This is the more true in so far as, in modernity, 'the state' does claim to 'represent' all, unlike its pre-capitalist forebears (although in England, again complicating Marx's portrayal of the past, this claim was being made routinely of Parliament from at least the fourteenth century). 'Mortall God', in short, has all too often turned out quite unashamedly to be a Protestant white man of property. Max Weber, arguing against Schmoller's claim that the state could be 'above' classes, was admirably clear-sighted when he referred to 'the state, *that is*, those groups which, under changing circumstances, by exercising political power dominate the nation' (cited in Mommsen 1977: 389). His observation applies not only to ruling classes, but to ruling genders, colours and creeds as well.

6

One way to summarize Marx's overview of the transition from 'the past' to modernity would be to say that it is a passage from the concrete and the particular to the abstract and universal. The canvas on which capitalism paints is that of the universal space-time which it, unprecedentedly, conjures into being, and within this unified globality abstraction rules. Time and again Marx uses the term 'abstract' in connection with the modern world. The 'cell-form' of this abstraction is the commodity form itself, with its extinction of use by exchange value, and behind that of concrete by abstract labour; a distinction, he says, that holds 'the whole secret' of his 'critical conception' (1868b). The duality of the commodity is clearly the template for his analysis of a wide variety of other bourgeois social forms: in particular, of those forms which both individuality and community assume within modern capitalist societies. In both instances concrete particularity is masked in abstract generality, with a resulting mystification. The qualitative and particular differences which concretely make individuals who they are appear inessential to them, while the generic equality which appears to characterize their subjectivity is abstract, formal and illusory. The 'ideal community' of the state is grounded in this denial of difference (whilst concretely regulating the relations which constitute it). Marx generically contrasts modernity and all that came before it in these terms. Thus feudalism, he considers, 'separates the human being from his general essence, [and] turns him into an animal that is directly identical with its function'. But 'the modern era, *civilization*, makes the opposite mistake. It separates the *objective* essence of the human being from him as merely something *external*, material. It does not accept the content of the human being as his true reality' (1843a: 81). The *Grundrisse* sums up his thinking when it asserts that 'individuals are now ruled by *abstractions* whereas previously they were dependent on one another' (1858: 101).

Marx is doing more than merely drawing analogies with the value form here. For him what is estranged as 'the economy' *is* a nexus of social relationships, the fundamental ones, he thinks, in modern life, and both the modern subject and the modern state are based in the social division of labour which gives rise to the commodity form. The 'abstract individual' emerges when what concretely constitutes individuals, their social relations, takes on the guise of things; the 'sheer, blank individuality' of the modern subject expresses the fact that the 'content of the human being' has become 'the plaything of alien powers' (1843b: 154). The value form can serve Marx as the paradigm of modern sociality because for him modern sociality actually *takes the form* of relations between commodities. The social world of capitalism appears as something we inhabit – Durkheim's society *sui generis* – rather than some ways we are, and it is this estrangement of the real content of social life that grounds the abstractions which come to stand in for it: modernity's representations (which is to say, its re-presentations) of both society and self.

It is this alienation rather than the mere rapidity of change (for which it is the prior condition) which underpins the transitory, fleeting and contingent experience so many have seen as the hallmark of the modern condition. As Marx paints it, for the modern individual sociality *has* become temporary, ephemeral, and accidental. Social relationships are no longer palpably the foundation of individuals' identities, while individuality is experienced as non-social, 'purely' personal. At least this is so, I would say, in those arenas of modernity where material life *is* produced in commodity forms, and individuals are fully equal juridical persons. Elsewhere women still leave their barons at inordinate personal cost, and Filipino nannies who offend their *patrones* risk summary deportation.

Nowhere is this derangement of personal and social more evident, for Marx, than in class. The latter, in fact, emerges as a highly problematic category. Marx sees 'free' wage-labour as *the* distinctive relation of the capitalist system, the *sine qua non* for the generalization of the commodity form itself. Beneath the ceaselessly changing surface of modern society, its 'everlasting uncertainty and agitation', hides the eternal return of the ever-same: 'the reproduction and new production of the *very relationship of capital and labour*, of *capitalist and worker*' (1858: 387; cf. Frisby 1985). But with this essential relation are reproduced, and ever produced anew, the abstractions implicit in the commodity form itself, the *Erscheinungsformen* in which modern sociality and subjectivity are represented. These furnish the daily source for 'the ordinary consciousness of the agents of production themselves' (1865a: 25), and they are, for Marx, wholly mystifying. Class, in short, is not the same kind of immediately experienced social reality as *Stand*, while those forms in which our sociality is represented concertedly obscure the relations which actually constitute it, class above all. Rulers, I would argue, can and do translate class into *Stand*, whether at Harrow or Hyannisport. But for the majority, the experience of modernity is profoundly contradictory. Individuals are perpetually riven between 'personal' experiences and public identifications, differences which cannot be represented, and representations which deny difference. What cannot readily be voiced, in this discourse, is above all the collectiveness of disadvantage, the sociality of subordination.

'Possession' of 'things' appears accidental and extrinsic to who individuals are, a mere accident of fortune, while the wage relation presents itself as a contract between free, equal and independent subjects, and – exactly like any other exchange of commodities – a fair exchange of equivalents. As Marx expresses it in a wonderfully sarcastic passage in *Capital*, 'only buyer and seller, mutually independent, face each other in commodity production.... Since sales and purchases are negotiated solely between particular *individuals*, it is not admissible to seek here for relations between whole social *classes*' (1867a: 586–7). He frequently contrasts the 'transparency' of pre-capitalist forms of exploitation with the opacity of wages. The labour of serf families on their plots and the lord's demesne are separated in time and space; not so the necessary and surplus labour of the modern wage-worker. The social productivity of combined labour – of, that is, the working class – meanwhile appears to be an inherent attribute of capital, whether in its avatar of self-expanding value (interest-bearing capital is where, for Marx, capital's 'relations ... assume their most externalized and fetish-like form' (1865a: 391)), or in its awesomely material incarnation as instrument of production. Thus is the 'essential relation' of the whole capitalist system (and with it, their own agency) comprehensively veiled to its subjects.

Exactly the society, then, whose basis is, for the first time in human history, class relationships (as distinct from 'relations of personal dependence') is *for this very reason* the society where realization of that fact seems least likely to occur. Or to put it more cautiously, much as capitalism must eternally reproduce the unequal foundations on which it rests, and with this, the concrete experience of subordination, it also renders that experience exceedingly difficult to articulate as anything other than contingent and private. This is inherent in the character of the class relationship itself, that which makes it, I have argued, so distinctively modern: its quality as a relation mediated by things rather than immediately inscribed in subjective identities. These mediations – commodities, money, capital – establish, to the contrary, the phenomenal basis for a pervasively 'abstract' set of representations of society and self which systematically deny class and other differences. This is not merely a matter of 'false consciousness' (a category which so far as I know Marx never used, indeed he could not consistently have done so). 'The way of looking at things', he argued against Hodgskin, 'arises out of the relationship itself' (1863, vol. 3: 295–6). Capitalism is a system less of self-deception, than of pervasively deceiving representations of self. Its foundation is that ideal being I have called the subject.

It seems, then, that *The Communist Manifesto*, with which I began, was a trifle premature in claiming that with the advent of capitalism, 'man is at last compelled to face, with sober senses, his real conditions of life, and his relations with his kind'. It may indeed be that capitalism 'has left remaining no other nexus between man and man than naked self-interest, than callous "cash payment"' (1848: 487), at least in that sphere it constitutes as 'the economy'. But there can be very little that is *more* mystifying than this 'cash nexus'. People's 'real conditions of life' and their 'relations with their kind' would seem to be exactly what is most obfuscated in a society ruled by 'the magic of money' (1867a: 92). As Marx portrays it, capitalism is 'an enchanted, topsy-turvy world', a veritable firmament of mirages (1865a: 830). In the light of this, let me raise a heretical question. Might it not be the case that what is most socially *consequential* in capitalism is not the class relation on which it rests, but the wider 'abstraction' of sociality and subjectivity entailed in the generalization of the commodity form which this relation makes possible – the revolution in the elementary forms of modern life which I have tried to trace here? It is time to turn to Max Weber, who argued something very like this, bringing what remains a sub-text in Marx to the none too comforting light of day.

Chapter three

The ghost in the machine

When I call in my labourers on a Saturday night to pay them, it often brings to my mind the great and general day of account, when I, and you, and all of us, shall be called to our grand and awful reckoning.... No repentance on the part of these poor men can now make a bad week's work good. This week is gone into eternity.

Hannah More, *The Two Wealthy Farmers* (quoted in Thompson 1967)

1

Capitalism, Max Weber says in his 'last word' on the subject, the course of lectures he delivered during the last year of his life since published under the title of the *General Economic History*, 'is present wherever the industrial provision for the needs of a human group is carried out by the method of enterprise', in other words, by private business (1966: 207). In his Introduction to the 1920 edition of *The Protestant Ethic and the Spirit of Capitalism* he offers a rather broader definition, which would encompass Marx's 'antediluvian forms' of merchants' and usurer's capital as well as 'industrial provision': a 'capitalistic economic action' is 'one which rests on the expectation of profit by the utilization of opportunities for exchange, that is on (formally) peaceful chances of profit' (1974: 17) – irrespective, he adds, of whether such a profit derives from trade or from manufacture.

On either definition capitalism is found in many societies. Trade 'can be traced back into the stone age' (1966: 232), and one can find many instances of enterprises run on capitalist lines, in the general sense of being oriented to the pursuit of profit, long before the modern era. Weber distinguishes other pre-modern forms of capitalism, not discussed by Marx: booty capitalism, adventurer capitalism, speculation in the spoils of political office, war financing, and so on (1974: 17–21; 1964: 278–80; 1966: Chapters 23, 26). But for him, as for Marx, the mere presence of capitalism in sectors of economic life does not suffice to make an entire economy or society capitalist. 'A whole epoch can be designated as typically capitalistic only as the provision of wants is capitalistically organized to such a predominant degree that if we imagine this form of organization taken away the whole economic system must collapse', and this 'is characteristic of the occident alone and even here has been the inevitable method only since the middle of the nineteenth century' (1966: 207–8).

The capitalism with which Weber is most concerned is this *'peculiar modern Western* form of capitalism', or 'sober bourgeois capitalism' (1974: 24), as he nicely describes it. This is as historically specific a phenomenon as it was for Karl Marx. Its distinctiveness, moreover, and contrary to a widespread Marxist misconception of Weber's views, lies as much in its organization of production. It is the continuous and rational employment of capital 'in a productive enterprise for the acquisition of profit, especially in industry' which is 'characteristically modern' (1968: 291). Bourgeois capitalism alone has 'produced a rational organization of labour, which nowhere previously existed' (1966: 232).

A 'rational capitalistic establishment', according to the *General Economic History*, 'is one with capital accounting, that is, an establishment which determines its income-yielding power by calculation according to the methods of modern bookkeeping and the striking of a balance'. 'Rational capital accounting as the norm for all large industrial undertakings which are concerned with provision for everyday wants' is therefore 'the most general presupposition for the existence of this present-day capitalism' (1966: 208), and it too 'has arisen as a basic form of economic calculation only in the Western World' (1964: 193). Weber lists six conditions which must be met for rational capital accounting to become the economic norm (1966: 208–9). Two of these closely correspond to Marx's fundamental social relations of capitalist production, division of labour on the basis of private property, and free wage labour.

Modern western capitalism, says Weber, 'involves ... the appropriation of all physical means of production – land, apparatus, machinery, tools, etc., as disposable property of autonomous private industrial enterprises', and this is a phenomenon which is 'known only to our time'. It also requires 'free labour'. He characterizes this as nakedly as does Marx:

> Persons must be present who are not only legally in the position, but are also economically compelled, to sell their labour on the market without restriction. It is in contradiction to the essence of capitalism, and the development of capitalism is impossible, if such a propertyless stratum is absent, a class compelled to sell its labour services to live; and it is likewise impossible if only unfree labour is at hand. Rational capitalistic calculation is possible only on the basis of free labour; only where in consequence of the existence of workers who in the formal sense voluntarily, but actually under the compulsion of the whip of hunger, offer themselves, the costs of products may be unambiguously determined by agreement in advance.
>
> (ibid.)

Also like Marx, Weber sees 'free labour' as having originally been recruited for the nascent capitalist industries 'by means of compulsion, though of an indirect sort'. He emphasizes the role played in England, the 'home of capitalism', by the Elizabethan Poor Law and Statute of Apprentices, regulating a population 'rendered destitute by the revolution in the agricultural system' with 'its displacement of the small dependent peasant by large renters and the transformation of arable land into sheep pastures', and highlights the way Justices of the Peace, down to the nineteenth century, 'exercised an arbitrary control over the labour force and fed the workers into the newly arising industries' (1966: 227–8). These were the same mechanisms of 'the so-called primitive accumulation' Marx discussed in *Capital* (1867a: Part 8).

In his Introduction to *The Protestant Ethic*, too, Weber maintains that 'exact calculation – the basis of everything else – is only possible on a basis of free labour'. He also goes so far as to aver that all of 'the other peculiarities of Western capitalism have derived their significance in the last analysis only from their association with the capitalistic organization of labour' (1974: 22). Wage labour is, then, just as fundamental to the modern world for Weber as it is for Marx – though for rather different reasons, as we shall see. It is also, as the prevalent form of labour, unique to modern capitalism. The 'rational capitalistic organization of (formally) free labour' is 'a very different form of capitalism [from its antecedents] which has appeared nowhere else' than in the modern West (1974: 21).

Weber's other four conditions (1966: 208–9) are 'rational technology, that is, one reduced to calculation to the largest possible degree'; 'calculable law', that is, 'law which can be counted upon, like a machine' (1966: 252); 'freedom of the market, that is, the absence of irrational limitations on trading'; and 'the commercialization of economic life', by which he means 'the general use of commercial instruments to represent share rights in enterprise, and also in private ownership', something which implies the 'further motif' of 'speculation'. The *General Economic History* also stresses two other key conditions for modern capitalism, absent from Weber's original six-point catalogue: 'the state in the modern sense, with a professional administration, specialized officialdom, and law based on the concept of citizenship'; and 'a rational ethic for the conduct of life'. Both of these are specific to the West, 'special features of its general cultural evolution which are peculiar to it' (1966: 232–3). *The Protestant Ethic* adds 'the separation of business from the household' (1974: 21–2), a crucial requirement on which I shall have more to say later. There is nothing in this list to which Marx would have been at all likely to take exception. But there are significant differences of emphasis. These are related to Weber's specification of rational capital accounting as the 'most general presupposition' of modern western capitalism.

2

'Rationalization' is a critical concept in Weber's work, to which I shall return: it is central to his analysis of the *differentia specifica* of modernity. Suffice it to say, in this context, that when he qualifies capitalism as rational he is referring, not to the substantive but to the formal rationality of economic action. Formal rationality is 'the extent of quantitative calculation or accounting' involved in such action. Substantive rationality is 'the degree to which a given group of persons ... is or could be adequately provided with goods' thereby, and here rationality is judged in accordance with 'a given set of ultimate values' (1964: 184–5). In *The Protestant Ethic* Weber makes it clear that the ethos either of 'labour as an end in itself' or of 'money-making as an end in itself, to which people were bound, as a calling' – imperatives he sees as 'characteristic elements of our capitalistic culture' – are substantively *irrational*, and indeed the object of that study is to seek the origin of this 'irrational element' in what he calls the 'spirit of capitalism' (1974: 63, 73, 78). What makes modern capitalism formally rational is not its ends but the unprecedented extent to which actions of economic agents are *calculated*. In this respect it is the apotheosis of that form of social action which Weber calls *Zweckrationalität*, that is, action in which 'the end, the means, and the secondary results are all rationally taken into account and weighed' (1964: 117).

Zweckrationalität contrasts with traditional action ('almost automatic response to habitual stimuli which guide behaviour in a course which has been repeatedly followed') and *wertrational* action (where an absolute end is pursued 'entirely for its own sake and independently of any prospects of external success'). In the latter case, although ends are consciously formulated and the courses of action rationally planned with a view to their attainment, these ends themselves are above calculation. Agents are morally obligated to pursue them unconditionally. Examples 'would be the action of persons who, regardless of possible cost to themselves, act to put into practice their convictions of what seems to them to be required by duty, honour, the pursuit of beauty, a religious call, personal loyalty, or the importance of some "cause" no matter in what it consists'. *Zweckrationalität*, by contrast, always involves some 'rational consideration of alternative means to the end, of the relations of the end to other prospective results of the employment of any given means, and ... of the relative importance of different possible ends' (1964: 115–18).

Capitalism, Weber says, is not identical with the 'impulse to acquisition', which 'exists and has existed among waiters, physicians, coachmen, artists, prostitutes, dishonest officials, soldiers, nobles, crusaders, gamblers, and beggars'. Capitalism indeed *'may* even be identical with the restraint, or at least a rational tempering, of this irrational impulse' towards 'unlimited greed for gain'. What distinguishes capitalism is 'the pursuit of profit, and forever *renewed* profit, by means of continuous, rational, capitalistic enterprise'. This entails 'calculations in terms of capital': and within a capitalist environment, Weber argues, any business enterprise which did not act thus 'would be doomed to extinction' (1974: 17). He concurs with Marx on the role of competition in disciplining individual capitals (and workers):

> the capitalistic economy of the present day is an immense cosmos into which the individual is born.... It forces the individual, in so far as he is involved in the system of market relationships, to conform to capitalistic rules of action. The manufacturer who in the long run acts counter to these norms, will just as inevitably be eliminated from the economic scene as the worker who cannot or will not adapt himself to them will be thrown into the streets without a job.
>
> (1974: 54–5)

But it is the orientation to action itself on which Weber chooses to focus. 'The important fact is always that a calculation of capital in terms of money is made.... Everything is done in terms of balances' (1974: 18). He records that the device of striking a balance, the symbol as much as the method of this calculation, was invented by the Dutchman Simon Stevin in the year 1698 (1966: 207).

It is as essential conditions for rational calculation that Weber's various presuppositions of modern capitalism assume their significance. As Collins (1986; cf. Weber 1964: 275–8) has noted, what Weber in fact theorizes are the key institutional conditions required by the market, as depicted by neo-classical economics. According to this view, the market provides optimal conditions of calculation for individual entrepreneurs. The information they require if they are to pursue profit in the most rational way is summated in prices, while prices can only fulfil this function if markets in goods, capital and labour are left to operate freely and competitively. Marx too argues (1867a: 73) that once the commodity form has become general, prices have 'to be taken into account, beforehand, during production'; the market compels calculation as an orientation to action on the part of individual producers. 'The highest degree of rational capital accounting', Weber maintains, hence 'presupposes the existence of competition on a large scale' (1964: 193). Private property in the means of production is thus critical because only under such conditions are they 'freely disposable', unlike, say, most land in medieval Europe. The most rational expression of this is representation of ownership rights by commercial instruments like shares, which can themselves be freely traded.

Similarly with wage labour: Weber did not subscribe to Marx's theory of surplus value. The significance of free labour is not that it is the exploited source of profit, but that it can be hired and fired, and its wages rise and fall, with demand, on the basis of criteria of efficiency alone. Only under these conditions is the fully rational calculation of costs possible for the individual enterprise. Additionally, Weber argues, the 'expropriation of workers from the means of production' allows for the 'unified control' of production, and with this comes 'the possibility of subjecting labour to a stringent discipline ... controlling both the speed of work and the standardization and quality of products'. Discipline is fundamental to predictable calculation, and 'free labour and the complete appropriation of the means of production create the most favourable conditions for discipline' (1964: 246–8).

Elsewhere Weber compares the large industrial enterprise to the army: 'military discipline', in his view, 'is the ideal model for the modern capitalist factory', and such discipline finds its incarnation in 'scientific management' (1968: 38). 'The maximum of formal rationality in capital accounting', he concludes, 'is possible only where the workers are subjected to the authority of business management', a type of management which (echoing Marx) he explicitly describes as 'autocratic'. Management can hire 'according to ability and willingness to work', fitting workers to tasks according to aptitude and motivation. The existence of guaranteed rights on the part of workers either to jobs, or to any participation in management, will produce 'technically, as well as economically, irrational obstacles to efficiency' – substantively irrational as this state of affairs might be from the point of view of the working class (1964: 247–8). In this sense the capitalist enterprise is a more (formally) rational economic arrangement than a producers' co-operative. Moreover, Weber points out, in a system of free wage labour 'the costs of reproduction and of bringing up children fall entirely on the worker', and 'largely for this reason, the risk of dismissal is an important incentive to the maximization of production' (1964: 277). Here, as more generally (see 1978a: Part 2, Chapters 3 and 4), he pays far more attention to the familial contexts of capitalism than does Marx, although he has comparatively little to say on the gender relations involved.

In the same way, the importance of mechanization lies not so much in its productive power as in the predictability it offers. For Weber, as for Marx, industrial technological development is a consequence rather than a cause of capitalism, and presupposes the existence of mass markets (which gave 'the decisive impetus toward capitalism') (1966: 230) and mass production on the basis of what Marx characterized as the formal subordination of labour to capital. In the case of law, likewise, Weber argues that what is critical is consistency. 'Formalistic law is ... calculable' (1966: 252), in a way that law based on 'material principles', justice which is substantial and therefore *ad hoc*, is not. Rational law in turn requires the modern bureaucratic state to secure 'a reliable formal guarantee of all contracts by the political authority' (1964: 275), and a plurality of nation states maintains the freedom of markets, as each 'compete[s] for mobile capital' (1966: 249). Anticipating Wallerstein (1974), Weber holds that 'it is the closed national state which afforded to capitalism its chance for development', and foresees that 'as long as the national state does not give place to a world empire capitalism will also endure' – an important insight (1966: 249).

The 'absence of irrational limitations on trading in the market', finally, is a self-evident requirement for any rational capitalism: for 'if a certain mode of life were prescribed for a certain class or consumption were standardized along class lines, or if class monopoly existed, as for example if the townsman were not allowed to own an estate or the knight or peasant to carry on industry [...] neither a free labour market nor a commodity market exists' (1966: 208). Full calculability presumes the 'complete absence of substantive regulation of consumption, production, and prices, or of any other forms of regulation which limit freedom of contract or specify conditions of exchange' (1964: 275). This is not the same as absence of regulation *per se*. Like Marx, Weber knew that the conditions under which such markets could operate were those of extensive social regulation, pre-eminently through the state: he is quite clear, for instance, that within modern capitalism 'the appropriation of the means of production by owners', one of his key conditions for free markets to operate, 'is protected by force' (1964: 262). I shall come back to the separation of household and enterprise, and Weber's most distinctive contribution to the sociology of capitalism, the 'rational ethic', later.

Weber agrees with Marx, then, on much of what substantively defines capitalism and makes it a specifically modern phenomenon, notwithstanding the different viewpoints (in brief, as a form of economic action as distinct from a mode of production) from which they approach its analysis. Their agreement extends well beyond the presuppositions of capitalism, into areas I have no space to develop here: one example is Weber's discussion in *General Economic History* of the development of industrial technique, which closely parallels Marx's in *Capital* (Weber 1966, Chapter 27; Marx 1867a, Part 4). But I cannot resist quoting the *Grundrisse*, written five years before Weber's birth (but only published long after his death), on one supposed bone of contention between the two men. 'The cult of money', Marx remarks there, 'has its corresponding asceticism, its renunciation, its self-sacrifice – thrift and frugality, contempt for the worldly, temporary and transient pleasures; the pursuit of *eternal* treasure. Hence the connexion of English Puritanism or also Dutch Protestantism with money-making' (1858: 164; cf. 1878: 60; 1867a: 593–4). No, this is not the full-blown 'Weber thesis'. But it should give pause for thought.

3

There are, however, differences, and not just of emphasis. Let me begin – mainly in order to get it out of the way – with what I regard, perversely, as the least important of these. This is the question of class. As every sociology undergraduate knows, Weber both defined class (in *Economy and Society*) differently from Marx, and identified two other major dimensions of 'social stratification', as the enduringly ugly language of sociology has it, 'status' and 'party'. Weber himself saw these, less blandly, as 'phenomena of the distribution of power within a community', power being a relationship, something the conventional geological metaphor conveniently obscures: 'the chance of a man or a number of men to realize their own will in a communal action even against the resistance of others who are participating in the action' (1970: 180–1). I will confine what I have to say here to 'class' and 'status', having suggested the reconcilability of Weber's views on party with Marx's already. 'The factor that creates "class"', according to Weber, 'is unambiguously economic interest', and specifically 'only those interests involved in the existence of the market' (1970: 183). Class is not, as for Marx, a relationship of exploitation, in the sense that Weber does not view capital itself as the product of surplus labour. He accepts that there are enduring *inequalities* of 'life chances' in modern capitalist society, but this is not quite the same thing.

We may speak of a 'class', Weber says:

> when (1) a number of people have in common a specific causal component of their life chances, in so far as (2) this component is represented exclusively by economic opportunities in the possession of goods and opportunities for income, and (3) [it] is represented under the conditions of the commodity or labour markets.

He argues (from the 'law' of marginal utility) that 'disposition over material property ... excludes the non-owners from competing for highly valued goods', and 'gives [owners] a monopoly to acquire such goods'. '"Property" and "lack of property" are, therefore, the basic categories of all class situations.' But 'within these categories ... class situations are further differentiated' for both owners and non-owners, 'on the one hand, according to the kind of property that is usable for returns; and, on the other hand, according to the kind of services that can be offered in the market' (1970: 181–2). Elsewhere (1968: 201ff.) Weber dubs the groups thus differentiated 'property classes' and 'acquisition classes' respectively.

Ownership of different kinds of property – e.g. land as against factories – differentiates the class situation of the propertied, who 'for instance, may belong to the class of rentiers or to the class of entrepreneurs'. Similarly with the non-propertied, who are 'differentiated just as much according to their kinds of services'. Although both are 'proletarians' in Marx's generic sense, for Weber an unskilled labourer and, say, a London printworker in the pre-Murdoch era would not occupy the same class situation. They enjoy very different life chances on the basis of the scarcity – whether 'natural' or 'artificial' – of their respective services on the market. And for Weber 'always this is the *generic* connotation of the concept of class: that the kind of chance in the *market* is the decisive moment which presents a common condition for the individual's fate'.

'"Class situation" is, in this sense, ultimately "market situation".' Weber adds, here, that 'naked possession *per se* ... is only a forerunner of real "class" formation', and those 'whose fate is not determined by the chance of using goods or services for themselves on the market, e.g. slaves' are not a class but a 'status group' (1970: 182–3). It is not possession (or lack of possession) of goods or skills as such which defines class, but the possibility of utilizing these in a market context. Weber's third criterion is critical. He sees class, in the strict sense of the word, as coterminous with the commoditization of property and labour: a state of affairs which finds its fulfilment only in modern capitalism. Where these markets are absent, so too are classes, as distinct from status groups.

From here Weber argues that 'the rise of societal or even of communal action from a common class situation is by no means a universal phenomenon'; 'however different life chances may be, this fact in itself, according to all experience, by no means gives birth to "class action"'. A common class situation 'may be restricted in its effects to the generation of essentially *similar* reactions', whether to what he calls 'mass action' – 'acts of an intermittent and irrational protest' – or 'merely an amorphous communal action'. What is critical to the likelihood of class action is 'general cultural conditions, especially ... those of an intellectual sort', and particularly important is 'the *transparency* of the connexions between the causes and the consequences of the "class situation"' (1970: 183–4). A class, Weber says, 'does not in itself constitute a community', although 'class situations emerge only on the basis of communalization'. The example of such 'communalization' he gives is an instructive one. It is that of the bourgeois state, which he describes as 'a specific kind of "legal order"' which is 'specifically structured to protect the possession of goods *per se*, and especially the power of individuals to dispose, in principle freely, over the means of production' (1970: 184–5). He echoes Adam Smith in his bald insistence that 'the modern economic order under modern conditions could not continue if its control of resources were not upheld by the legal compulsion of the state; that is, if formally "legal" rights were not upheld by the threat of force' (1964: 160). But Weber's overall point here is reminiscent of E. P. Thompson's contention that class struggle precedes class. He maintains that 'the communal action that brings forth class situations ... is not basically actions between members of the identical class; it is an action *between* members of different classes' (1970: 185).

If class, for Weber, is exclusively an economic matter, 'status' is 'determined by a specific, positive or negative, social estimation of *honour*', and 'status honour is normally expressed by the fact that above all else a specific *style of life* can be expected from all those who wish to belong to the circle'. Unlike classes, status groups usually are communities, and various forms of 'closure' on social intercourse – e.g. on residence, or marriage – both typify them and are mechanisms in their constitution. 'Usurpation' is 'the normal origin of almost all status honour' (1970: 186–8). Status may be sedimented in legal privilege, as in medieval estates, or, as with the extreme case of castes, is ritualized and sanctified by norms of purity and pollution. Weber notes that ethnic segregation may form the basis for the development of status groups, but does not see this as usual; rather, 'very frequently a status group is instrumental in the production of a thoroughbred anthropological type' (1970: 190). 'Ethnicity', in other words, may itself often be *constructed* by social power; he instances legal and informal prohibitions on cross-'racial' marriages in the post-bellum US South (1978a: 386). It is, Weber says, typical among privileged strata that 'there is a status disqualification that operates against the performance of common physical labour', while 'very frequently every rational economic pursuit, and especially "entrepreneurial activity", is looked upon as a disqualification of status' (1970: 191) – a facet of status which is clearly at odds with the ethos of capitalism. In fine, for Weber '"classes" are stratified according to their relations to the production and acquisition of goods; whereas "status groups" are stratified according to the principles of their *consumption* of goods as represented by special "styles of life"' (1970: 193).

Understandably, Marxists have rarely been much enamoured of Weber's analysis of stratification. Most fundamentally, as they see it, he omits any conception of a relationship between capital and labour other than that of the contingent nexus of the market. Exploitation – for Marx what capital accumulation *is* – simply disappears. Labour and capital, as Marx said of the 'trinity formula' of 'vulgar economics' – which was for him 'the complete mystification of the capitalist mode of production' – 'do not stand in any hostile connection to one another because they have no inner connection whatsoever' (1863, vol. 2: 503). The most one can say, from a Weberian standpoint, is that the bourgeoisie as a collectivity employs the state and the 'legal order' it maintains to secure conditions in which the market advantages attendant upon private property ownership are perpetuated. Additionally, Weber's concept of class fractures the unity of both capital and labour, with obvious implications for Marxist expectations of apocalyptic class conflict, while his treatment of status and party as independent dimensions of social power muddies the waters still further by suggesting 'non-economic' foundations for inequality. On the question of exploitation there remains an unbridgable gulf between Marx and Weber, which reflects the very different economic theories – respectively, classical political economy and marginalism – upon which their sociologies of capitalism are predicated. How important this is, I would argue, is debatable: both men recognize the same basic conflict of class interests as fundamental to bourgeois society. But as for the rest, altogether too much ink has been wasted over their supposed differences.

Weber is quite clear that – in the market context – it is ownership or otherwise of property which is the fundamental axis of class position; and this, as we have seen, is reflected in his insistence that private property in the means of production, and the existence of a 'propertyless stratum' of free labourers, are essential conditions for modern capitalism. He accepts that free markets systematically work to the advantage of capital, and is under no delusions whatsoever as to the 'equality' of the various contracting parties: 'possession of property', he says, gives to management 'bargaining superiority ... both on the labour market in relation to the worker, and in the commodity market' *vis-à-vis* 'any competitor ... less well situated with respect to capital and credit resources' (1964: 248). Marx, conversely, is equally clear that both the bourgeoisie and the proletariat are, as social classes, internally fragmented, and the basis for this is the division of labour – in other words, that which determines differing market opportunities for individuals. I have amply documented this above. Marx's own empirical studies, notably *The Eighteenth Brumaire*, distinguish numerous 'class fractions', who emerge as the real subjects of his historical narratives. The supposed 'two-class' model of capitalist society ascribed to him by the authors of sociology textbooks (and drawn largely from the *Manifesto*) is most conspicuous by its absence (1852).

Marx, like Weber, saw the formation of a class 'for itself' (Weber's 'class action') from a class 'in itself' (Weber's 'class situation') as problematic, and regarded the 'transparency' of class relations as a major difficulty. Why else did he expend so many words on the illusoriness of the wage contract? He thought the development of capitalist production would promote a class consciousness on the part of workers, notwithstanding his acute awareness of capitalism's propensity to mystify its underlying relations. This may have been overly optimistic. But Weber too considered 'the class situation of the modern "proletariat"' to be 'the most important historical example' of a class situation in which 'the contrast of life chances can be felt not as an absolutely given fact to be accepted, but as a resultant from ... the structure of the concrete economic order'; one of two kinds of circumstance in which 'people may react against the class structure ... in the form of rational association', as distinct from sporadic protest (1970: 184). Marx contrasted peasant revolts with working-class movements in similar terms (whether accurately, in the light of twentieth-century experience of peasant revolutions from Mexico to Vietnam, is another issue) (1852: 187–8). 'Rational socialism' was for Weber also unique to the modern West, and its basis, as for Marx, was 'the rational organization of free labour under regular discipline' (1974: 23), 'bondage to the machine and regular work discipline' (1978b: 252).

Weber's stress on the importance of 'cultural conditions ... of an intellectual sort' for the development of a consciousness of class curiously echoes Marx's own observation that modernity is characterized by 'individuals being dominated by ideas' (as it does also Georg Simmel's contention that, as David Frisby puts it, 'the extension of the money economy and the domination of the intellect ultimately coincide' (Frisby 1985: 80)). Both Marx and Weber provide grounds for thinking that the modern world is uniquely conducive to the emergence of political ideologies which take as their object both the analysis and the transformation of societies as totalities, like socialism. The condition for this is precisely the abstraction of the social. Kautsky and Lenin were to define the role of communist parties in terms of making transparent to the working class its 'true' social position, so as to transform its spontaneous 'trade union consciousness' into real 'political consciousness'. The source of the latter, says Lenin (quoting Kautsky), is 'the *bourgeois intelligentsia* ... [hence] socialist consciousness is something introduced into the proletarian class struggle from without' (1902: 383). It is on such grounds that Communist Parties have justified their 'leading role', and slaughtered their peoples to defend it, from Kronstadt to Timisoara. This was, it should be said, by no means Marx's own position, but it is a comprehensible enough way of resolving the contradictions in the experience of class which his work does anatomize.

Marxist criticisms of Weber's views on status usually come

down in essence to the assertion that status is (as they say, 'in the last instance') merely a function of class. Two things need to be said here. First, Weber himself was clear that 'property as such is not always recognized as a status qualification, but in the long run it is, and with extraordinary regularity' (1970: 187). The *parvenu* may 'never [be] accepted, personally and without reservation, by the privileged groups', but descendants will be, by virtue of the culture property can buy (1970: 192). Weber acknowledges that 'today the class situation is by far the predominant factor' in the formation and membership of a status group, 'for of course the possibility of a style of life expected for members of a status group is usually conditioned economically' (1970: 190). Conversely, there is ample warrant in Marx's analysis of the contradictions of modern subjectivity for expecting differences of occupation, consumption and lifestyle to become the foundation for the elaboration of status distinctions within the class polarities of modernity. Class, I have argued, is for Marx rarely experienced directly for what it is, while the subjective impact of capitalism's multiple divisions of labour is immediate and palpable.

The second point, however, is the more important. I argued above that for Marx class as such is a peculiarly modern social relationship. Its foundation is capitalism's transmutation of personal relations into relations mediated through things. It is only property in commodities – the commodities which for Weber confer market opportunity, capital and labour – which defines class, and such property is a distinctively modern phenomenon, at least as the basis of the social and economic order. Now Weber concurs in this: slaves did not for him form a *class* because they had nothing to sell on a *market*. Recall here Marx's citation of Justinian. Sociologists have (as is their custom) thoroughly dehistoricized Weber's notions of class and status, treating them as analytic components of any social order. It is true that in *Economy and Society* Weber is establishing 'pure' ideal-types which no real society perfectly exemplifies. This, incidentally, holds for 'rational capitalism' too, as well as for bureaucracy, which I shall examine below. This is an elementary precaution against taking abstract concepts as immediately descriptive of empirical realities, a vice to which Marxists and Weberians alike are all too prone (Sayer 1987). But

Weber is also very clear that class is pre-eminently a phenomenon of modernity. 'In the past', he says, 'stratification by status was far more decisive [...] for the economic structure of the societies', whereas 'present-day society is predominantly stratified in classes' (1970: 301).

Weber opposes class and status in ways not dissimilar to Marx's own distinction between class and estate; indeed the term translated in Weber's writings as 'status group' (*Stand*) is the same as is translated in Marx's case as estate. 'The market and its processes', Weber holds, *'"knows no personal distinctions"'* – for Marx the 'groundwork' of all pre-capitalist societies – for '"functional" interests dominate it. It knows nothing of "honour".' With the organization of society along lines of status, on the other hand, 'the market is restricted, and the power of naked property *per se*, which gives its stamp to "class formation", is pushed into the background' (1970: 192–3). 'Status groups', Weber says, 'hinder the strict carrying through of the market principle', because, in brief, their 'closure' withholds specific goods from free exchange (1970: 185). The essential principle of status is monopolization. For Weber, just as for Marx, status hierarchies – Marx's 'feudal, patriarchal, idyllic relations' – are therefore inimical to the principles of modern capitalism, and capitalism erodes them (if less comprehensively than Marx himself sometimes implied). Weber posits a correlation between a situation of stability in 'the bases of the acquisition and distribution of goods' (which as we have seen was for Marx the economic norm within the pre-capitalist world of cyclical reproduction) and status as the major dimension of the social order; and he powerfully echoes the *Communist Manifesto* in asserting that 'every technological repercussion and economic transformation threatens stratification by status and pushes the class situation' – Marx's 'cash nexus' – 'into the foreground' (1970: 193–4).

The question of exploitation aside, what is most significant here is surely the extent of agreement between Marx and Weber on what class is, how it differs from pre-modern social relations, and its centrality to modern, capitalist society. The obverse of this, also common to both, is a neglect of other differences in modern societies like 'race' or gender, which in fact are not readily comprehensible in terms either of class or *Stände* as either theorist conceives them. These are not seen by Weber or Marx as in any sense intrinsically related to capitalism, and capitalism is accepted by both as the basis of the modern social order.

4

Let us now turn to some more substantial differences between these two thinkers. Marx's avowed object in *Capital* was 'to lay bare the economic law of motion of modern society' (1867a: 10). But Weber had other concerns entirely. The proper framework in which to place his analysis of capitalism is the question he poses at the beginning of his Introduction to *The Protestant Ethic*:

> A product of modern European civilization, studying any problem of universal history, is bound to ask himself to what combination of circumstances the fact should be attributed that in Western civilization, and in Western civilization only, cultural phenomena have appeared which (as we like to think) lie in a line of development having *universal* significance and value.
>
> (1974: 13)

Otherwise put – though much in Weber's 'line of development' is age-old – this is the problem of modernity. Weber parades an impressive array of cultural phenomena distinctive, he thinks, to 'Western civilization', which reach their zenith only in modern times. The thread linking them is the idea of rationalization: something which, for Weber, may be epitomized in capitalism, but is neither confined to it nor originates with it. It needs, I think, to be said at once that Weber's contentions here, as with Marx's blanket portrayals of the 'childish' pre-capitalist world, are more than disputable. Weber's discourse is as ridden with Orientalism as Marx's, and he appears oblivious to the degree to which the very notion of a distinctive 'occidental' tradition (against which all that is Other can be generically homogenized and contrasted) is itself a modern creation, and one not wholly unconnected with capitalism's global expansion (Bernal 1987). 'Traditions' are constructed, not least through the kinds of coherence given retrospectively to history by accounts like Weber's (and Marx's) own.

What we might begin to recognize as 'Occidentalism' (a designation I borrow from my friend Philip Corrigan) is as much an artefact as its Oriental Other, a space-time of the mind. As Teodor Shanin (1984) once observed, on this projection North America is Europe, while Bulgaria is not.

'Only in the West', Weber argues, 'does science exist at a stage of development which we recognize today as valid.' Other forms of knowledge, highly developed as they were, were merely empirical, not rational: Babylonian astronomy lacked mathematical foundation (furnished by the Greeks), Indian geometry rational proof (also a product of 'the Greek intellect'), Indian natural science the method of experiment ('essentially a product of the Renaissance'), Indian medicine a biological and particularly a biochemical foundation ('a rational chemistry has been absent from all areas of culture except the West'). Chinese historical thought 'did not have the method of Thucydides', Indian political theory 'was lacking in a systematic method comparable to that of Aristotle, and, indeed, in the possession of rational concepts'. Law, even if codified in the Near East, nowhere exhibited 'the strictly systematic forms of thought, so essential to a rational jurisprudence, of the Roman law and of the Western law under its influence. A structure like the canon law is known only to the West.' Weber argues similarly of music, art and architecture. 'Rational harmonious music', with its orchestras, symphonic and operatic forms, and system of notation 'are known only in the occident'; likewise the 'rational use of the Gothic vault', and 'the rational utilization of lines and spatial perspective', a gift, again, of the Renaissance. Though printing was known in China (and earlier, let it be said, than in Europe), a literature designed only for print – above all, the press and periodicals – is uniquely western. Even if the East managed to come up with 'philosophical and theological wisdom of the most profound sort', 'the full development of a systematic theology must be credited to Christianity under the influence of Hellenism' (1974: 13–15).

Turning from *mentalités* to institutions, Weber sounds the same refrain. Chinese and Islamic academies are 'superficially similar to our universities', but 'a rational, systematic, and specialized pursuit of science, with trained and specialized personnel, has only existed in the West'. We come here to a key motif in Weber's thought. The 'trained official', he argues, 'a type of which there have heretofore only been suggestions, which have never remotely approached its present importance for the social order', is 'the pillar of both the modern State and of the economic life of the West'. Officials were known in 'the most various societies':

> But no country and no age has ever experienced, in the same sense as the modern Occident, the absolute and complete dependence of its whole existence, of the political, technical, and economic conditions of its life, on a specially trained *organization* of officials. The most important functions of the everyday life of society have come to be in the hands of technically, commercially, and above all legally trained government officials.
>
> (Weber 1974: 15–16)

Even 'the feudal state of *rex et regnum* ... has only been known to our culture'; still more so elected parliaments and government by responsible ministers. Indeed, Weber maintains, 'a political association with a rational, written constitution, rationally ordained law, and an administration bound to rational rules or laws, administered by trained officials, is known ... only in the Occident' (1974: 15–16); 'the rational state has existed only in the western world' (1966: 249). So have both professional politicians and lawyers as a professional status group (without whose 'juristic rationalism, the rise of the absolutist state is just as little imaginable as the Revolution') (1970: 94).

The same, he argues in *General Economic History*, holds for the concept of citizenship: 'the notion of citizens of the state is unknown to the world of Islam, and to India and China', while the 'social class signification of citizen as the man of property and culture ... in contrast with the nobility, on the one hand, and the proletariat, on the other, is likewise a specifically modern and western concept, like that of the bourgeoisie' (1966: 233–4). Compare Marx, who opines of modern citizenship 'it should read: domination of the bourgeoisie' (1846a: 215). Indeed for Weber 'the city in the strict sense' is itself 'specifically a western institution', in that 'outside the occident there have not been cities in the sense of a unitary [political] community' (1966: 238, 235). The city

plays a key role for Weber in the history of western culture. It 'created the party and the demagogue', 'brought forth the phenomenon of the history of art' and alone 'produced science in the
modern sense'. It was 'the basis of specific religious institutions' –
Judaism, Christianity and Protestantism, he claims, were all quintessentially urban phenomena – and was the cradle both of theology *and* 'thought untrammeled by priestcraft'. Peasants were never
in a position materially to obey the Judaic law (while priests were,
for Weber, the first specialists of the intellect). Cities were also
'the seat of commerce and industry', requiring 'a continuous provision of the means of subsistence from without' (1966: 234–5).

Weber explains the distinctiveness of the western city, its character as a *polis* in which citizens came under its law and partici-
pated in the choice of its administrative officials, by two other
specifically occidental peculiarities. The first is the nature of its
provision for defence. 'Whether the military organization is based
on the principle of self-equipment or on that of equipment by a
military overlord who furnishes horses, arms, and provisions', he
claims, 'is a distinction quite as fundamental for social history as
is the question of whether the means of production are the
property of the worker or of a capitalist entrepreneur' – a preg-
nant parallel, to which I shall return. Western cities were initially
organizations for defence of the former kind: the ultimate origin
of citizenship lies in 'the *coniuratio*, the brotherhood in arms for
mutual aid and protection'. But elsewhere 'the development of the
city was prevented by the fact that the army of the prince is older
than the city', something which in turn, as for Marx, who described
Asiatic cities merely as 'royal camps' (1858: 406), was grounded in
'the question of irrigation'. This 'hydraulic society' thesis, which
was to be taken to its extreme by Wittfogel (1957), is another
hardy perennial of Orientalist wisdom. But Weber draws a major
historical contrast here, which does not wholly depend upon the
irrigation argument. 'In the west ... the separation of the soldier
from the paraphernalia of war, in a way analogous to the separation of the worker from the means of production, is a product of
the modern era' – it happens only in the modern state – 'while in
Asia [this] stands at the apex of the historical development' (1966:
236–7). This conception of a great original divide between the

'western' and the 'Asiatic' paths of social development was of course also, if for rather different reasons, Karl Marx's.

Weber's second 'obstacle to the development of the city in the orient', one wholly consonant with his general theme of western rationalism, is 'ideas and institutions connected with magic'. Indian castes are 'ceremonially alien to one another', no basis for *coniurationes*. In western antiquity, by contrast, the priests had no monopoly over communion with the gods; civic officials performed rites (and, claims Weber, priestly offices were sometimes vulgarly filled by auction). Judaic prophecy, and subsequently Christianity, with its proselytizing fellowship with the uncircumcised, later broke down remaining 'magical barriers between clans, tribes and peoples ... and the establishment of the modern city was made possible' (1966: 338).

5

And then, of course, there is capitalism, at the same time 'the most fateful force in modern life' (1974: 17), and but one instance among others of this more wholesale rationalization of western culture and institutions. I indicated above why for Weber capitalism is the acme of *Zweckrationalität*: nowhere is 'the end, the means, and the secondary results' of action more 'rationally taken into account and weighed' than in the fine calculations of the modern enterprise. *Zweckrationalität* is in fact merely cost-benefit calculation writ large, the mode of orientation to action of *homo economicus*, and capital accounting furnishes the paradigm for its analysis. Capitalism is not, however, its cause. Weber does not regard 'the rational spirit, the rationalization of the conduct of life in general and a rationalistic economic ethic' (1966: 260) as mere by-products of the rise of capitalism. Rather it presupposes them – along, it should be emphasized, with very much else beside (see Weber 1974: 92–3, 183, 266).

What needs explanation, then, is the origin of this 'spirit' or 'ethos'. We should be quite clear here that Weber is by no means the idealist he is so often portrayed as (any more than Marx was a crude materialist). He was quite categorical that 'not ideas, but material and ideal interests, determine men's conduct'. He did believe, however, that 'very frequently the "world images" that have been created by "ideas" have, like switchmen, determined the tracks along which action has been pushed by the dynamic of interest' (1970: 280). This was the case, he thought, with the rationalistic ethic of modern capitalism. Herein lies Weber's major disagreement with 'the materialist conception of history', as he encountered it. He defined this as a 'dogmatic need to believe that the economic "factor" is the "real" one, the only "true" one and the one which "in the last instance is everywhere decisive"'. It is a fair enough summary of much *fin de siècle* Marxism, if (in the light of much posthumously published material unavailable to Weber) a travesty of Marx, for whom, as we have seen, the very separability of an 'economic factor' is a modern product. Weber said just about all that is necessary on such 'materialism' in four incisive pages of his 1904 essay on '"Objectivity" in Social Science', which ought to be required reading for all Marxists (1949: 68–71). He cuts through a century of Ptolemaic contortion, from Engels to Althusser, like a knife through butter. The important point, however, for our purposes, is that Weber was crystal clear that he did not intend, even in his apparently most 'idealistic' text *The Protestant Ethic* (which this disclaimer closes) 'to substitute for a one-sided materialistic an equally one-sided spiritualistic causal interpretation of culture and of history' (1974: 183).

Rationalization, as the notion has emerged so far, in Weber connotes systematicity, consistency, method: whether as a cast of mind, or as the principle on which organizations are structured, it implies the exclusion of arbitrariness and above all of what he refers to as 'magic'. Rationality amounts to the calculated application of rules. Its antithesis is 'traditionalism', which, Weber maintains, 'lies at the beginning of all ethics and the economic relations which result' (1966: 260). Traditionalism is 'the psychic attitude-set for the habitual workaday and ... the belief in the everyday routine as an inviolable norm of conduct' (1970: 296). He famously illustrates a typically traditionalist economic attitude by the Silesian agricultural labourer who, having had his wages doubled, promptly halved his work (1966: 260–1). This is Marx's pre-capitalist world of 'the traditional satisfaction of existing needs' with a vengeance.

For Weber such traditionalism is the 'leading trait of precapitalist labour'. It may be intensified by two kinds of circumstance; where 'material interests' – e.g. the 'special interests of officials, landholders and merchants' – are 'tied up with the maintenance of tradition'; or through 'stereotyping of trade on magical grounds, the deep repugnance to undertaking any change because supernatural evils are feared' (1966: 261). He gives the well-known example of the problems of constructing railroads in China: geomancy, he says, 'demanded that in the location of structures on certain mountains, forests, rivers, and cemetery hills, foresight should be exercised in order not the disturb the rest of the spirits'. Caste barriers were similarly a major obstacle to establishing capitalism in India, where 'workmen who dare not accept a vessel filled with water from each other's hands, cannot be employed together in the same factory room'. 'Obviously', he concludes, 'capitalism could not develop in an economic group thus bound hand and foot by magical beliefs' (1966: 265; on caste, cf. 1970: 411–14).

Also characteristic of traditionalism, and a roadblock in the way of rationalization, is an 'originally universal dualism of internal and external moral attitudes':

Internally, there is attachment to tradition and to the pietistic relations of fellow members of tribe, clan, and house community, with the exclusion of the unrestricted quest of gain within the circle of those bound together by religious ties; externally, there is absolutely unrestricted play of the gain spirit in economic relations, every foreigner being originally an enemy in relation to whom no ethical restrictions apply; that is, the ethics of internal and external relations are categorically distinct.

(Weber 1966: 260–1)

Neither of these attitudes will serve for rational capitalism, which requires, on the one hand, 'the bringing in of calculation into the traditional brotherhood, displacing the old religious relationship', and on the other, 'a tempering of the unrestricted quest for gain' which as we have already seen Weber in no way equates with capitalism. As did Marx (and Simmel), he links the disintegration of 'the native piety and its repression of the economic impulse' with

the breakdown of 'communistic' economic relations, and this is
once again a 'development ... especially characteristic in the West'
(1966: 260–1). This evidently meshes with Marx's picture of the
modern world as comprising sovereign individuals who are 'mutually indifferent', and relate to one another on the moral basis of
the exchange of equivalents. Marx, incidentally, did not view capitalism as being devoid of ethical foundations; as he put it, 'every
social form of property has "morals" of its own', and 'Political
Economy expresses moral laws *in its own way*' (1871: 505; 1844:
311).

In the West itself, however, it is for Weber 'a peculiar fact' that
'officially a theory was dominant which was ... in principle strongly
hostile to capitalism'. This 'theory' was, of course, Christianity.
Both Catholic and Lutheran ethics were antipathetic to 'every capitalistic tendency'. Not only did the Church abhor usury; 'medieval
economic ethics excluded haggling, overpricing and free competition, and were based on the principle of a just price and the assurance to everyone of a chance to live', or in other words upon a
substantive rationality. The origin of this, Weber argues – again
powerfully echoing Marx's characterizations of the pre-capitalist
social world – was 'repugnance to the impersonality of relations
within a capitalist economy'. Where a master/slave relation 'could
be subjected to immediate ethical regulation', 'the relations between a mortgage creditor and the property which was pledged for
the debt, or between an endorser and the bill of exchange, would
[be ...] impossible to moralize' (1966: 262–3). But despite this, for
Weber, it was exactly Christianity – or more accurately, the Judeo-
Christian heritage – which was to prove the decisive agency of
western rationalization, the 'switchman' which pushed the dynamic of interest in a fateful direction. And within Christianity,
especially consequential for capitalism was ascetic Protestantism,
by which Weber means above all Calvinism, together with Pietist,
Methodist and Baptist sects.

6

Here I must summarize a long and complex argument developed
in a variety of texts. *The Protestant Ethic*, written in 1904–5, is *not*

Weber's last word on the topic. In his *General Economic History* of 1920, he argues that 'great rational prophecy' – that is, the utterances of a prophet 'who furnishes credentials in the shape of miracles and otherwise' – is a means of 'breaking down the power of magic and establishing a rational conduct of life'. 'Prophecies', he claims, 'have released the world from magic and in so doing have created the basis for our modern science and technology, and for capitalism.' Ancient Judaism developed such prophecy to an extent not found elsewhere, and both Judaism and Christianity are (relatively) free of magic – particularly in Christianity's Protestant form with its hostility to the doctrine of salvation by works. But the Eucharist already 'sublimated magic into the form of a sacrament' which is a means neither of guaranteeing salvation nor of evading damnation. As importantly, Judaism and Christianity, in contrast to the 'ascetic religions of salvation of India', are resolutely 'plebeian' religions – they do not, as Weber claims Buddhism does, reserve their higher 'ethical precepts' for 'a thin stratum of monks' who prophesy by example alone. Within the Judeo-Christian world (and again above all in ascetic Protestantism, which rejected the distinction between religious virtuosi and laity that remained central to Catholicism) 'magic was suppressed among the population to the greatest possible extent'. It was 'reduced to the character of something unholy, something diabolic' (1966: 265–7). God is not persuadable by trickery and hocus pocus, rather these demean His majesty.

One consequence of this (at least after the Reformation) is that His world becomes morally accessible to rational scientific enquiry; God's glory is manifest in the laws of Nature. Durkheim too, in his magisterial *Elementary Forms* (1976), advanced the heretical proposition that the roots of scientific thought lie in religion, though for reasons somewhat different from Weber's. Keith Thomas, writing of the 'single all-directing Providence' of Protestantism (and acknowledging Weber), suggests 'a religious belief in order was a necessary prior assumption upon which the subsequent work of the natural scientists was to be founded' (1978: 786). A pertinent contrast can be found in Paul Veyne's portrait of the deities of classical antiquity (1987: 207–19): they formed part of the natural order of things, not its very principle. They could therefore love, hate, sin and be bribed, palliated and bargained with. This is not the 'ordered and rational universe' (Thomas 1978: 786) which goes along with the Protestant conception of an omnipotent and omniscient Creator. Such divinities were capable of caprice.

This said, we should perhaps recall also that the ancient Greeks' word for the universe, *cosmos*, means order, while it was a Christian mob who sacked the greatest scientific library of the ancient world, at Alexandria. Monotheism in itself has hardly proved everywhere to be a necessary, or anywhere a sufficient, condition for the development of a rational-scientific outlook. Such objections, however, if anything strengthen the case Weber and Keith Thomas make for the specific import for science of the Calvinist God. The post-Reformation admixture of religiosity and science produced some (to us) bizarre outcomes. Christina Larner (1981) argues, for example, that the great European witch-hunts were no survival of 'traditionalism', but an application of rationalized legal procedures intimately linked to modern state formation, while Isaac Newton himself, as Thomas documents, dabbled in alchemy and endeavoured mathematically to compute the date of the apocalypse. Both nonetheless were in Weber's sense eminently rationalized, methodic endeavours.

Simmel argues a related case regarding Christianity. 'A God of the Universe', he says, has to be intolerant of the gods of others; 'any allegiance to other gods is a positive infringement on the ideal claim He asserts by His absolute monopoly'. The Christian deity – an unprecedentedly militant, proselytizing version of the monotheistic conception not bound by any covenant with a specific chosen people – 'was the first to break through the exclusiveness of the social group, which until then had dominated all the interests of its members with its own unity of space and time' (1959: 68–9). This is a nice counterpart of the universal space-time of a world history which Marx claims is first brought into being with modern capitalism. Although Simmel is speaking of Christianity in general, one might venture that it was the Protestant Reformation which gave to such a conception its most consistent form. Catholicism was (and is) far more tolerant of the religious observances – though not necessarily the beliefs –

of others, often incorporating them syncretically into its own ceremonials.

7

But the core of Weber's argument, to my mind at least, lies in the case he makes for a specific subjectivity being engendered by the Reformation. This is a new kind of individuality, one that is uniquely fitted to the norms of 'sober bourgeois capitalism'.

Asceticism, he argues, *is* (formally) rational in that it prescribes 'a definite, methodical conduct of life'. In medieval European Christendom 'the monk is the first human being who lives rationally, who works methodically and by rational means toward a goal, namely the future life. Only for him did the clock strike, only for him were the hours of the day divided – for prayer'. The Church, Weber also remarks, 'furnished officialdom for the early middle ages' (the word clerk has the same root as cleric). But the Reformation transformed this ascetic ideal, decisively. In breaking with the 'dualistic ethic' of one code of conduct for religious virtuosi and another for followers, Protestantism took the methodicality of the monastery (and the convent) out into the everyday, mundane world – 'you think you have escaped from the monastery, but everyone must now be a monk throughout his life' (1966: 267–8). Protestantism thus 'gave *everyday* worldly activity a religious significance'. Henceforth 'the only way of living acceptable to God was not to surpass worldly morality in monastic asceticism, but solely through the fulfilment of the obligations imposed upon the individual by his position *in* the world': and this changes everything (1974: 80).

Peter Brown has made a similar case for the lay Christian communities of late western antiquity, contrasting them with the monastic foundations of the Eastern Mediterranean, and luminously exploring the radical implications for the civic signification of the individual body (in Veyne 1987: Chapter 2). In the case of Protestantism, Weber argues, the consequence was that 'the moral conduct of the average man was ... deprived of its planless and unsystematic character and subjected to a consistent method for conduct as a whole' (1974: 117). In this novel 'inner worldly asceticism', an ethic no longer of rejection of the world but of conduct *within* it, we can begin to discern the outlines of the modern subject, Descartes' *cogito* (or, come to that, Freud's supposedly universal trinity of Ego, Superego and Id), eternally looking over the shoulder and into the conscience, monitoring the 'I' and its conduct. This is what Foucault (1988) has called a new technology of the self. Weber employed a remarkably similar language. He speaks, more than half a century earlier, of the 'perfecting of the self' (1968: 272).

A key text for Weber's understanding of modernity, which among other things makes it very clear that for him the legacy of inner-worldly asceticism for modern subjectivity is a lasting one, is his essay on American Protestant sects (1970: 302–22). Indeed for him, as for Marx (who described the United States as 'the most modern form of bourgeois society' (1857: 40–1)), the new world of North America came to epitomize modernity, its soaring sky-scrapers the 'fortresses of capital' (1970: 15). In this essay, which draws on Weber's personal experiences touring the US in 1904, he makes the crucial point that in terms of its social implications 'it is not the ethical *doctrine* of a religion, but that form of ethical conduct upon which *premiums* are placed that matters'. In the case of the Puritan sects 'that conduct was a certain methodical, rational way of life which – given certain conditions – paved the way for the "spirit" of modern capitalism'. Premiums were placed on '"proving" oneself before God in the sense of attaining salvation', and '"proving" oneself before men in the sense of socially holding one's own within the Puritan sects' (1970: 321). As *The Protestant Ethic* makes clear, to prove oneself before God was not a magical means of attaining grace, but rather a method of confirmation that one was worthy of grace, which was in His almighty gift.

Wealth acquired morally, Weber (contentiously) argues there, perversely came to be interpreted as a 'sign of election' to those who had surrendered to the 'magnificent consistency' of Calvin's doctrine of predestination. Only the saved, it was reasoned, would prove spiritually capable of living the kind of disciplined life which would reap them such earthly rewards. This doctrine, Weber contends, cannot but have have led to 'a feeling of unprecedented inner loneliness of the single individual' (1974: 98–115). Simmel too remarks that 'the God of Christianity is the God of the individual.... The individual stands before his God in absolute self-reliance' (1959: 67), and as we have seen, Marx also commented on Christianity's *'cultus* of abstract man'. Might one perhaps extend this to suggest that the modern individual is constituted *as* so singular and isolated a subject by such means? Weber suggests that we indeed can.

Protestantism, he points out, expected of its adherents, not the recurring (and, he maintains, the 'very human') cycle of sin, confession and absolution accepted by the older Catholicism, but a *continual* ethical 'probation'; 'the God of Calvinism demanded of his believers not single good works, but a life of good works combined into a *unified system'* (1974: 115). The godly were perpetually on trial. Morality is thereby abstracted from all particularistic contexts, becoming an ontological attribute of the *subject* rather than of his or her discrete *actions*, and it provides the basis upon which this new subjectivity is unified. Weber contrasts an ethic of good works in which 'particular actions [...] can be evaluated singly and credited to or subtracted from the individual's account', as exemplified in the Hindu doctrine of *karma*, Zoroastrianism, Judaism and (in its practice) Roman Catholicism, with what he calls the 'ethic of inwardness' characteristic of Protestantism. In the former, human behaviour is 'more than a simple and uniform quality of personality, of which conduct is the expression'. A given action has to be located in terms of its *intentio*. In the latter, by contrast, individual actions are treated as being the 'symptoms and expressions of an underlying ethical total personality', and it is this total personality which becomes the object of 'ethical rigorism'. The consequence is that 'religious good works with a social orientation become mere instruments of *self-perfection'* (1968: 271–2).

This is a profound transformation, in which the ethical becomes, in the phraseology of the nineteenth century, a question of *character*, a core constituent of personal identity. The self thus constructed has the attributes Marx also ascribed to the modern subject: internal coherence and detachment from all social particularity, a 'pure, blank individuality' naked to the gaze of the all-seeing God. Such a persona also becomes susceptible to improvement (which in the heroic phase of capitalism used to be written with a capital 'I'): 'a religious total personality pattern may be envisaged as something which may in principle be acquired through training in goodness'. Such training, it goes without saying, comprises 'a rationalized, methodical direction of the entire pattern of life, and not an accumulation of single, unrelated actions' (1968: 272). The affinities between this portrayal of the Protestant personality and Michel Foucault's exploration (1977) of how modern technologies of discipline work on a reorganized subjectivity are plain. The sect, for Weber, operated very much like a Panopticon.

The requirement of ethical consistency was reinforced by the obligation to prove oneself before one's peers. In Catholicism and Lutheranism, moral discipline was exercised by the priest in authoritarian fashion, but in Puritan sects it was in the hands of the laity. It was enforced not through the ritual and public penances of ecclesiastical courts, but 'through the necessity of having to hold one's own; and ... it bred or, if one wishes, selected qualities'. Demonstration of ethical fitness was both a condition of acceptance into the sects (unlike for the universal church, into which one is born) and something that had repeatedly to be proven if individuals were to 'hold their own' within them. The contrast with the Catholic practice of confession, for Weber, is striking: 'confession of sins was ... a means of *relieving* the person from the tremendous internal pressure under which the sect member in his conduct was constantly held' (1970: 320). The rite of confession was also, I would suggest, a means of reintegrating the acknowledged sinner into a position in a religious community accepted as subordinate. The Catholic hierarchy is patriarchal; the penitent confesses to a father. The internal pressure of the sect, on the other hand – if it was survived – cultivated, if not the sin of pride, then certainly a strong sense of individual self-worth, of moral rectitude: a standing among equals. The sects bred a 'formalistic, hard, correct character which was peculiar to the men of that heroic age of capitalism' (1974: 166). Weber suggests that 'the ascetic's humility ... is always of dubious genuineness' (1968: 280). It is a telling insight, when applied to those who possessed, in their assurance of grace, the self-confidence to remodel the world in their own image.

Puritan discipline, Weber maintains, thus 'put the most powerful individual interest of self-esteem in the service of this breeding
of traits. Hence *individual* motives and personal self-interests
were also placed in the service of maintaining and propagating the
"bourgeois" Puritan ethic' (1970: 321), because 'admission to the
congregation is recognized as an absolute guarantee of the moral
qualities of a gentleman, especially of those qualities required in
business matters' (1970: 305). One wonders whose qualities, befit-
ting them for which activities, were required of Protestant women,
but Weber does not say. Sect membership, in short, is tantamount
to a moral credit rating. A further consequence of this requirement of ethical probity was to break down the dualistic economic
ethic of traditionalism: 'the Godless cannot trust each other
across the road; they turn to us when they want to do business;
piety is the surest road to wealth', Weber quotes (1966: 269).
Again we meet Marx's motif of universalization, now as an inter-
nalized norm of ethical conduct. The benefits of such an attitude
to 'sober bourgeois capitalism' are obvious enough.

8

On the question of discipline and 'a strictly regulated, reserved
self-control' (1974: 173), Weber anticipates much that is central
to the work of Elias (1982) and Foucault, though neither of these
thinkers would link these quintessentially modern qualities so
uniquely to Protestantism. For Weber the ascetic 'will always
demand of the world an ethically rational order and discipline,
corresponding to his own methodical self-discipline', and this may
entail 'a revolutionary transformation of the world for this purpose' – the purpose of 'an unconditional subordination of the
world to the norms of religious virtue' (1968: 281). The object of
this discipline is elimination from everyday life of whatever is not
godlike, and 'the primary ungodlike factors were actually the average *habitus* of the human body and the everyday world, as those
are given by nature' (1968: 275), 'the spontaneous enjoyment of
life and all it had to offer' (1974: 166). Marx's attitude to nature,
as something to be subdued, is worth recalling here: it evokes,
albeit in a secularized form, the comprehensive ethic of mastery of

the world, the flesh and the devil, that Weber is depicting. 'Man', Marx believed, ought to be 'elevated' as the 'sovereign of Nature', including human nature. Remember that he wrote these words in an apologia for European colonialism. For Weber, as for many others of his generation, such a Promethean vision raised Nietzschean perplexities. The price of such human mastery over circumstances and self (as Marx put it) may be the denial of the life force which is its source. Simmel, in his later essays, was to write this conflict large as the ineluctable 'tragedy of culture' (1968).

In the Puritanical disciplining of the body, according to Weber, we again witness the transformation of the ascetic impulse into a code of conduct within the everyday world: 'celibacy was not required, marriage being viewed simply as an institution for the rational bringing up of children. Poverty was not required, but the pursuit of riches must not lead one astray into reckless enjoyment' (1968: 268). There is a far subtler transformation of sexuality here than is often recognized. Puritanism, as Weber portrays it, does not simply repress sexual impulse so much as routinize it, in ways which render particular constructions of human sexual identities natural, normal and moral. Here, as in other areas of his writing, Weber foreshadows some of Foucault's arguments (1980). A perfect example of this (not used by Weber himself) is furnished in the radical Puritan poet John Milton's treatment of sexuality in *Paradise Lost*, a work which sets out to 'assert eternal providence, and justify the ways of God to men' (Book 1, 25–6).

Paradise Lost paints Eve's beauty in language which is unashamedly sensual, and allows the parents of humanity to know one another before The Fall. Sexual enjoyment is not the fruit of eating from the forbidden Tree of Knowledge. Eve, Milton tells us, 'as a veil, down to the slender waist/Her unadorned golden tresses wore/Dishevell'd, but in wanton ringlets wav'd', and 'yielded' to Adam 'with coy submission, modest pride/And sweet reluctant amorous delay' (Book 4, 304–11). The two were soon 'imparadis'd in one another's arms', he 'in delight, both of her beauty and submissive charms', to 'enjoy their fill of bliss on bliss' (ibid.: 497–507); 'nor turn'd ... Adam from his fair spouse, nor Eve the rites mysterious of connubial love refused' (ibid.: 741–3). Milton certainly did not consider these 'rites' 'unbefitting holiest place, perpetual fountain of domestic sweets', indeed he attacks 'hypocrites' who 'austerely talk/Of purity, and place, and innocence/Defaming as impure what God declares/Pure' (ibid.: 743–60). Certainly he was 'advanced' in this contention, and Weber cites more representative Puritan sources in which any physical enjoyment of sex whatsoever is seen as a sinful legacy of The Fall (1974: 263–4). But Milton also considered 'discipline' to be 'not only the removal of disorder, but if any visible shape can be given to divine things, the very visible shape and image of virtue'. It was the 'axle' upon which 'the flourishing and decaying of all civil societies [...] are moved to and fro' (quoted in Hill 1964: 218). There is no contradiction here. Sexuality, like everything else, can be rationally ordered in a manner pleasing to God, that is Milton's point. It is also Weber's.

'Inner-worldly and rational asceticism', Weber maintains, 'can accept only the rationally regulated marriage' and must 'reject every sophistication of the sexual into eroticism as idolatry of the worst kind'. What is proscribed is neither sex nor even its enjoyment as such, but a 'consciously cultivated' enjoyment, a 'turning away from the naive naturalism of sex' of the kind Milton celebrates. The essence of eroticism, which is why it is anathema to asceticism, lies in its 'non-routinized' character of proffering 'a gate into the most irrational and thereby real kernel of life, as compared with the mechanisms of rationalization'. Through reducing sexuality to (what is claimed to be) its 'natural and organic basis' Puritanism integrates and controls it within a 'new and progressively rationalized total life-pattern' (Weber 1978a: 607). Indeed, as in *Paradise Lost*, the sexual becomes susceptible to a positive moral evaluation: Milton calls 'wedded love' – by which he clearly intends sexual love – the 'sole *propriety* in Paradise of all things else' (Book 4: 751–2). For Weber, 'this asceticism gathers the primal, naturalist, and *un*sublimated sexuality of the peasant into a rational order of man as creature' (1970: 243–50); sexuality too becomes a part of the seamless text of character, safely embraced within the wider ordering of the undivided moral personality. In *The Protestant Ethic*, he comments on how this vision prefigures the nineteenth-century medicalization of sexuality within a new discourse of 'hygienic utilitarianism'. 'For the

Puritan the expert was the moral theorist, now he is the medical man', but 'the claim of competence' with regard to determining 'healthy' sexuality 'is [...] the same in both cases' (1974: 263–4). The 'natural' locus of this reformed sexuality was, of course, the monogamous (and heterosexual) marriage, which finds its essential legitimation in 'the thought of *ethical* responsibility for one another' (1970: 349–50). The explosive potential of 'the greatest irrational force of life: sexual love' (1970: 343) is neutralized by this ethicization, its inclusion in 'a category heterogeneous to the purely erotic sphere' (1970: 350), and the condition for this is the construction of a particular 'unsublimated' sexuality as 'natural'; that is to say, Divinely ordained.

This rational ordering involved the submission of wives to the authority of their husbands, something that Milton also makes plain. Adam and Eve were each fashioned in 'the image of their glorious Maker', 'though both not equal':

> For contemplation he, and valour form'd,
> For softness she, and sweet attractive grace,
> He for God only, she for God in him:
> His fair large front and eye sublime declar'd
> Absolute rule ...

> (Book 4, 292–301)

Eve accepts that her 'beauty is excell'd by manly grace, and wisdom, which alone is truly fair' (ibid.: 490–1). 'My author and disposer', she says to Adam, 'what thou bidd'st/Unargued I obey: so God ordains; God is thy law, thou mine: to know no more/Is woman's happiest knowledge, and her praise' (ibid.: 635–8). But what has since been called the 'companionate marriage' also, says Weber, allows a new form of personal intimacy, which at its best (he instances the Quaker William Penn's letters to his wife) may be 'genuinely humane', 'a mutual granting of oneself to another and the becoming indebted to each other' (1970: 350). Despite its 'prudery', Puritanism can claim some 'positive accomplishments' in this domain. 'Matrimonial chivalry' supplants 'patriarchal sentimentality', and through 'the protection of her freedom of conscience, and the extension of the idea of the universal priesthood to her' Baptist influences, especially, 'have played a part in the emancipation of woman'. These doctrines were, Weber claims, among the first modern 'breaches in patriarchal ideas' (1974: 264).

Around the subject, then, grows up a protective cocoon, a newly constructed (and highly valued) 'domestic' realm which is counterposed to the impersonal world outside, mitigating the existential loneliness of modernity. In some of Weber's writings, notably 'Science as a vocation', this sphere of domestic sweets is also the last resort of simple human decency in an increasingly mechanized cosmos. I have suggested above that this model family's place in the social reproduction of the conditions under which capitalism has so far operated is much more pivotal than classical sociologies have been apt to recognize. The particular ethicization of the sexual remarked by Weber – there have, of course, been others – and with it, a specific gendering of subjectivities and restructuring of 'relations of personal dependence', whose moral fundaments are precisely *not* those of market contingency, would seem to me to be a critical element in this. These could be seen as part of that 'new storey beneath historical materialism' which Georg Simmel thought it necessary to uncover, asserting that every 'economic structure' itself had 'ideal depths' (1978: 56).

In the same way, Weber tells us, Puritans were not hostile to sport, 'if it served a rational purpose, that of recreation necessary for physical efficiency. But as a means for the spontaneous expression of undisciplined impulses, it was under suspicion'. Hence the significance of the struggle, in seventeenth-century England, over the *Book of Sports* (which allowed various profane amusements on the sabbath). Nor did 'the ideals of Puritanism impl[y] a solemn, narrow-minded contempt of culture'. But in so far as theatre, painting or literature – or 'the enjoyment of the dancehall or the public house of the common man' – smacked of 'idle talk, of superfluities, and of vain ostentation, all designations of an irrational attitude without objective purpose' they were taboo; and 'this was especially true in the case of decoration of the person, for instance clothing' (1974: 167–9). What are tellingly referred to in North America today as 'leisure activities' (among which the perfection of the self through physical exercises, nicely termed 'workouts', stands out; dieting, a practice now generalized within an organizing discourse of total bodily 'fitness' is arguably part of the same secular mortification of the flesh) were thus also deemed capable of rationalization. Implied is a cultural revolution of enormous systematicity and range, encompassing the minutiae of everyday life. Nothing was too trivial for such reforming earnestness, because everything had taken on a religious significance. This is a totalizing doctrine with far-reaching consequences for the individual's conduct in its every detail. Actions are read as being symptomatic of character, and discipline encompasses, and unifies, the whole personality.

In this, others since Weber have pointed out, Protestantism foreshadows another seminal feature of modernity, and we return, from another vantage-point, to Marx's (and Durkheim's) equation of moral individualism and state formation. 'From the late fifteenth century', Christina Larner has argued, 'the evangelization of the populace coincided with the development of what can loosely be called nation states.' These required of their subjects 'both ideological conformity and moral cleansing': a revolution of the heart, rather than merely ritual obeisance. Post-Reformation Christianity, both Protestantism itself and the systematized Counter-Reformation Catholicism renascence which it provoked, was, she claims, 'the world's first political ideology' (1982: 35–6). Weber's disciplined subject is the moral ground upon which modern forms of power are constructed, and, conversely, these in turn come to regulate what subjectivity is permitted to comprise. As Adam Seligman has pointed out (1990), the location of 'society' as the fount of moral authority is found first in the democratic and egalitarian Protestant sects (specifically, he argues, in the polities of New England). He portrays these as totalitarian in their behavioural demands on individuals. Weber's observation, à propos modern capitalism, that 'the Puritan wanted to work in a calling; we are forced to do so' (1974: 181) applies much more generally.

Un foi, un roi, une loi or *cujus regio ejus religio* mark a novel relation between the subject and power, within which what is now demanded of the former is an internalization of the ideological lineaments of the latter, so that they become the governing norms of conduct, core components of personal identity. Marx touched on this, speaking of the way '"vocation, destiny, task, ideal"' are 'set up as a standard of life ... partly as an embellishment or realization of domination, partly as a moral means for this domination' (1846a: 472–3). Bryan Turner, who criticizes Weber for failing to recognize the degree to which Protestantism's interpretation of the Doctrine of the Fall legitimated not only subordination of women and other social inequalities, but also 'state violence', is none the less only extending what is implicit in Weber's own 'characterology' when he argues that if we are to understand European state formation in its decisive period, we require 'a new concept, namely the nation-church-state' (1988: 330). Weber himself was not, however, wholly unaware of these connections. Though he noted the 'anti-authoritarian tendency' of Puritan asceticism (1974: 167) in *The Protestant Ethic*, later he was equally to stress that 'normally, Protestantism ... absolutely legitimated the state as a divine institution and hence violence as a means' (1970: 124).

9

If Protestantism's greatest contribution to capitalism – and the modern world more generally – lay in its breeding of the modern subject (which I think is the overall thrust of Weber's argument across his writings), it also furnished capitalism with specific ethical foundations which were, he is emphatic, substantively *irrational*. Since this territory, that of *The Protestant Ethic*, is well known, I shall be briefer. At the heart of the 'spirit of capitalism', he argues, lie two peculiar moral imperatives. These are 'the duty of the individual toward the increase of his capital, which is assumed as an end in itself', and 'the conception of labour as an end in itself, as a calling' (1974: 51, 63). Neither are natural, nor even readily comprehensible, and Weber stresses their oddity:

> In fact, the *summum bonum* of this ethic, the earning of more and more money, combined with the strict avoidance of all spontaneous enjoyment of life, is above all completely devoid of any eudaemonistic, not to say hedonistic, admixture. It is thought of so purely as an end in itself, that from the point of view of the happiness of, or utility to, the single individual, it appears entirely transcendental and entirely irrational. Man is dominated by the making of money, by acquisition as the ultimate purpose of his life. Economic acquisition is no longer

subordinated to man as the means for the satisfaction of his material needs. This reversal of what we should call the natural relationship, so irrational from a naive point of view, is evidently as definitely a leading principle of capitalism as it is foreign to all peoples not under capitalistic influence.

(1974: 53)

Marx too identified this 'reversal' as characteristic of modern capitalism, and contrasted antiquity and modernity in precisely the same terms, as we have seen. But what Marx treated simply as a consequence of capitalism, structurally imposed on capitalist and worker alike by their mutual alienation, is for Weber 'what really needs explanation' (1974: 55).

For him social action is what it is only by virtue of the meanings people place upon what they are doing, and 'subjective understanding' of these meanings is 'the specific characteristic of sociological knowledge' (1964: 104). Weber by no means held that Protestantism 'caused' capitalism. The latter was for him the product of a long and very complex chain of contingencies, ably reconstructed by Randall Collins (1986). But it is, he maintains, the social ethic of ascetic Protestantism which 'stood at the cradle of the modern economic man' (1974: 174), the subject of this very peculiar and intensely moral economy.

The affinities between the Protestant ethic and the 'spirit of capitalism' are legion. Protestantism, from Luther onwards, gives mundane activity religious significance. Work becomes a calling, the way through which one glorifies God. What matters is not *what* one does, but the *spirit* in which one does it. This, as the hymn puts it, 'makes drudgery divine'. There is, as I remarked above, a certain abstraction of labour involved here; it is Marx's 'expenditure of simple labour-power', precisely without distinction or hierarchy of its concrete forms, which is valued. In Weber's words, Puritanism esteemed 'labour in the service of impersonal social usefulness' (1974: 109); this is a democracy of toil. Time is similarly moralized: 'waste of time is ... the first and in principle the deadliest of sins', since 'every hour lost is lost to labour for the glory of God' (and since it has moral value, it is minutely reckoned). This is not yet Benjamin Franklin's maxim 'time is money'; but, as Weber delicately puts it, 'the proposition is true in a certain spiritual sense' (1974: 157–8). 'Work hard in your calling' is the fundamental Protestant prescription, recommended by Baxter (together with a vegetable diet and cold baths) also as a reliable antidote to the devil of sexual temptation (1974: 159).

Labour – that formerly despised activity and estate – is now a *duty*, from which the wealthy are least exempt. This is a 'perfect' middle-class morality, in terms of which both the idle poor and the idle rich are equally deserving of condemnation. If 'begging, on the part of one able to work, is not only the sin of slothfulness, but a violation of the duty of brotherly love', then 'the superior indulgence of the *seigneur* and the parvenu ostentation of the *nouveau riche* are equally detestable to asceticism' (1974: 163). Hill (1961), Thompson (1968) and others have stressed that this capability of Protestantism to confer respect – and respectability – on the everyday activities of the 'middling sort' (and indeed, as with Methodism, of the 'labouring poor') was one reason for its widespread appeal in a society already moving in the direction of capitalism. This emancipatory aspect of Protestant character is perhaps somewhat underplayed by Weber, as are its democracy, individualism and anti-authoritarianism, points also made by Hill and Tawney (1938). But their emphases are by no means incompatible with Weber's own. Arguably it is exactly the self-confidence nurtured by its self-discipline which made Protestantism the devastating social force it became. These are two sides of the same moral reconstruction of the self. To be Foucauldian about it (but this is exactly the burden of Weber's essay on the Protestant sects), the discipline of Protestantism not only restrains individuals, it also – and for the same reasons – empowers them; albeit, conveniently for capitalism, in differential and differentiating ways.

Protestantism's 'emphasis on the ascetic importance of a fixed calling', Weber argues, 'provided an ethical justification of the modern specialized division of labour' (1974: 163) and – where The Word was heeded (an accomplishment, I think, Weber sometimes far too readily takes for granted) – furnished the entrepreneur with 'sober, conscientious and unusually industrious workmen, who clung to their work as to a life-purpose willed by God' (1974: 177). These days we have secularized the calling as the 'career' (as in 'two-career family'), a designation which indissolubly marks the individual's temporal passage through the world in terms of the (waged) labour he or she performs. This inscription of one's place in the social division of labour as a moral signifier contrasts shockingly with ancient or medieval attitudes towards the distinctions of gentility. *Not* to work was formerly the badge of elevated status. Regarding capitalism's inequalities, Weber says, the entrepreneur had 'the comforting assurance that the unequal distribution of the goods of this world was a special dispensation of Divine Providence, which in these differences, as in particular grace, pursued secret ends unknown to men' (ibid.). God moves in a mysterious way, his wonders to perform. What matters is that one has faith, and labours diligently in one's appointed station, eschewing equally Giant Despair and Vanity-Fair. The story of Job provides the paradigm for virtuous conduct, a blueprint of character.

If labour is a calling, its fruits – property – are a trust. The entrepreneur is a steward of God's gifts, labouring to increase them for His glory. The parable of the talents is emblematic here. 'The greater the possessions the heavier ... the feeling of responsibility for them, for holding them undiminished for the glory of God and increasing them by restless effort.' Such an attitude 'had the psychological effect of freeing the acquisition of goods from the inhibitions of traditionalistic ethics. It broke the bonds of the impulse of acquisition in that it not only legalized it, but ... looked upon it as directly willed by God.' The Protestant idea of the calling 'gave the entrepreneur a fabulously clear conscience', so long as the profits of enterprise – a term, like 'industry' itself, that is deeply imbued with moral resonance – were not idly dissipated in vainglorious self-indulgence. Weber notes that 'against the glitter and ostentation of feudal magnificence which ... prefers a sordid elegance to a sober simplicity', Protestants 'set the clean and solid comfort of the middle-class home as an ideal' (which again raises the question of women's place in all this) (1974: 170–1).

'When the limitation of consumption is combined with this release of acquisitive activity', he suggests, 'the inevitable practical result is obvious: accumulation of capital through ascetic compulsion to save' (1974: 172). Marx's competitive '"March, march!"' thus has its psychological counterpart in an orientation to action which is obsessive, a compulsion of a different sort. All in all, Weber concludes, Protestantism's 'religious valuation of restless, continuous, systematic work in a worldly calling ... must have been the most powerful conceivable lever for that attitude toward life which we have here called the spirit of capitalism' (ibid.), and in comparison with as 'powerful, unconsciously refined [an] organization for the production of capitalistic *individuals*' as the ascetic Protestant community, 'what the Renaissance did for capitalism shrinks into insignificance' (1966: 270, my emphasis).

One final point is in order. Once securely established, Weber argues, capitalism can dispense with its former religious underpinnings. Indeed, he maintains, the rationalization which capitalism brings in its train is in general subversive of all religious orientations to earthly conduct. Mandeville's cynical and worldly *Fable of the Bees* is a more appropriate text for modernity. It is very important to stress this: for Weber 'the religious root of modern economic humanity is dead; today the concept of the calling is a *caput mortuum* in the world'. He suggests that together with this passes the 'consolation' which Protestantism once offered to workers, and thereafter 'it was inevitable that those strains and stresses should appear in economic society which have since grown so rapidly'. 'Economic ethics', then, 'arose against the background of the ascetic ideal', but now, in the 'age of iron', capitalism 'has been stripped of its religious import' (1966: 270). Weber's portrait of 'victorious capitalism' is closely akin to Karl Marx's in its characterization of a system which has become estranged from all human agency. 'Today', he contends, 'material goods have gained an increasing and finally an inexorable power over the lives of men as at no period in history.' Capitalism triumphant rests on purely 'mechanical foundations' (1974: 181–2).

But this does not mean the analysis I have recounted here can be dismissed as of merely historical interest. The valuation of the pursuit of wealth and the moralization of labour are still for Weber 'characteristic elements of our capitalistic culture'. So, I would suggest, is his compelled and compulsive individual the continuing 'subject' of bourgeois society. Severed from the religious integument which once gave them meaning, these are the ghosts in the machines of modernity.

Chapter four

Without regard for persons

The world, which seems,
To lie before us like a land of dreams,
So various, so beautiful, so new,
Hath really neither joy, nor love, nor light,
Nor certitude, nor peace, nor help for pain;
And we are here as on a darkling plain
Swept with confused alarms of struggle and flight,
Where ignorant armies clash by night.

Matthew Arnold, 'Dover Beach'

1

It is rationalization, then, not capitalism *per se*, which for Weber lies at the root of the modern world order, and the reasons for this are to be found in various peculiarities of 'the West'. Capitalism is but one theatre among others in which the drama of rationality is played out; and all the leading motifs of modern capitalism have their exact counterparts in many other arenas of social life. But if, for Weber, capitalism is no longer Marx's demiurge of modern society, it continues to furnish him with the paradigms through which modernity is analysed. Not only is it the major agency of global rationalization, capitalism is also the template in terms of which the overall social consequences of rationalization are comprehended. In this sense it remains the keystone of his general sociology of the modern world.

Thus, as we saw above, Weber draws a parallel between the separation of the worker from the means of production and the separation of the soldier from 'the paraphernalia of war'. Marx said that this 'severance of the conditions of production, on the one hand, from the producers, on the other, forms the *conception* of capital' (1865a: 246). For Weber, such severance is a feature of modern social organization across *all* spheres of life: 'this whole process of rationalization, in the factory as elsewhere, and especially in the bureaucratic state machine, parallels the centralization of the material implements of organization in the discretionary power of the overlord' (1968: 39). The beginnings of the modern state lie in 'the expropriation of the autonomous and "private" bearers of executive power ... who in their own right possess the means of administration, warfare, and financial organization'. 'The whole process' of state-making, Weber says, 'is a complete parallel to the development of the capitalist enterprise through gradual expropriation of the independent producers' (1970: 82). In effect he generalizes Marx's model of alienation, with the result that capitalism becomes a special case – if a uniquely 'fateful' one – of a more encompassing 'expropriation' which is the foundation of the discipline which sinews the modern subject into the 'machines' of modern society. Severance of the material means of a given human activity from its agents (which, just as for Marx, implies their isolation as solitary individuals) is the generic basis for all institutional rationalization. This is the key principle of that bureaucracy which for Weber pervades most arenas of modern life, capitalism included, and in bureaucracy we have discipline's 'most rational offspring', its perfected social form (1968: 29).

In 'modern officialdom', says Weber, there are 'fixed and official jurisdictional areas, which are generally ordered by rules, that is, by laws or administrative regulations'. Regular activities of the bureaucratic structure are 'distributed in a fixed way as official duties', as is the authority to command the discharge of these duties; and the exercise of this authority is 'strictly delimited by rules' concerning the sanctions officials may employ to secure compliance with their orders. This pattern is typical of 'bureaucratic authority' in the public domain and of 'bureaucratic management' in the private, and is respectively 'fully developed ... only in the modern state and ... only in the most advanced institutions of capitalism. Permanent and public office authority, with fixed jurisdiction, is not the historical rule but rather the exception.' Pre-modern rulers worked through 'personal trustees, table-companions, or court servants', and commissions of authority were 'not precisely delimited' in their scope, and *ad hoc* rather than permanent. Within this new unified jurisdictional space there is a clear, and hierarchical, division of labour and responsibility, 'a firmly ordered system of super- and subordination in which there is supervision of the lower offices by the higher ones' (1970: 196–7).

The essence of all such bureaucratic discipline is 'the consistently rationalized, methodically trained and exact execution of the received order, in which all personal criticism is unconditionally suspended and the actor is unswervingly and exclusively set for carrying out the command' (1968: 28). Specifically, Weber emphasizes, 'the discipline of officialdom refers to the attitude-set of the official for precise obedience within his *habitual* activity, in public as well as private organizations', and 'this discipline increasingly becomes the basis of all order, however great the practical importance of administration on the basis of the filed documents may be'. It is 'the settled orientation of *man*' – that is, of *modern* 'man' – 'for keeping to the habitual rules and regulations' that is the foundation of this *neue Ordnung* (1970: 229). Bureaucracy rests on the reorganization of *habitus*. Weber argues that such 'mechanization' is facilitated by a guaranteed salary and the opportunity of 'a career that is not dependent upon mere accident and arbitrariness'; working in the same direction are 'status sentiment among officials', and 'the purely impersonal character of office work' (1970: 208). The individual bureaucrat, unable to 'squirm out of the apparatus in which he is harnessed', is thus 'forged to the community of all the functionaries who are integrated into the mechanism' (1970: 228).

Officials, whether employees of private businesses or state servants, undergo 'thorough and expert training'. 'Educational certificates' are 'linked with qualifications for office', which enhances the 'status element' in the position of the official (1970: 198, 200);

'more and more the specialized knowledge of the expert became the foundation for the power position of the officeholder' (1970: 235). 'The system of rational, specialized, and expert examinations', Weber maintains, 'is increasingly indispensable for modern bureaucracy', and 'capitalism, with its demand for expertly trained technicians, clerks, et cetera, carries such examinations all over the world' (1970: 240–1). This valuation of technical expertise is radically different from the ideal of the 'cultivated man' which 'formed the basis of social esteem in such various systems as the feudal, theocratic, and patrimonial structures of domination' (1970: 243) – an esteem which rested on the gentleman precisely not being tied to a career but being an 'amateur', one whose means gave him the leisure to cultivate the self in ways that would enhance the public good. Weber clearly regrets the passing of this ideal; in the famous words of *The Protestant Ethic*, modernity turns the world over to 'specialists without spirit, sensualists without heart'; and 'this nullity', he scathingly writes, 'imagines that it has attained a level of civilization never before achieved' (1974: 182). Within the developed bureau, there is no room for gentlemanly amateurs: where previously 'official business was discharged as a secondary activity', nowadays 'official activity demands the full working capacity of the official'. Otherwise put, 'office holding is a "vocation"' and 'the position of the official is in the nature of a duty' (1970: 198–9).

In so far, Weber remarks, as this discipline appeals to any 'firm motives of an "ethical" character, it presupposes a "sense of duty" and "conscientiousness"' (which contrasts sharply with moralities of 'honour') (1968: 29). The functioning of the amoral 'machine' of bureaucracy thus rests, paradoxically, on a striking moralization of the individual's relation to it. The morality is one of subservience, of abnegation of individual responsibility; it is the morality demonstrated repeatedly at the Nürnberg trials. Weber summarized it well:

> the honor of the civil servant is vested in his ability to execute conscientiously the order of the superior authorities, exactly as if the order agreed with his own conviction. This holds even if the order appears wrong to him and if, despite the civil servants' remonstrances, the authority insists on the order.

He insists that 'without this moral discipline and self-denial, in the highest sense, the whole apparatus would fall to pieces' (1970: 95). This is exactly the same moral discipline and self-denial we encountered in the last chapter in the very different context of the Puritan sects, and reinforces the connection I drew there between this subjectivity and specifically modern forms of power.

Anticipating much subsequent writing on documentation as a critical modality of power, Weber highlights the fact that 'the management of the modern office is based upon written documents ("the files"), which are preserved', and associated with this is 'a staff of subaltern officials and scribes of all sorts' (1970: 197). More recent work has stressed the ways in which individual identities (as, for instance, a voter, taxpayer, driver, married person or schoolchild – all of them statuses 'licensed' by such recording practices) are comprehensively regulated thereby. Philippe Ariès has remarked a very material connection between modern subjectivity and state documentation: it is impossible, today, to survive in the world without knowing one's exact date of birth, something, for most people, which was rare before the eighteenth century (1962: 15–16). Our date of birth has become part of our civic identity (and what used to be called the 'ages of man' are marked by institutional *rites de passage*, from kindergarten graduation to mandatory retirement). Weber himself places more emphasis, as we might expect, on the purely technical advantages that rationalized documentation brings to the exercise of power.

He also emphasizes another, for him equally novel facet of bureaucracy, which is that the 'bureau' is 'in principle ... separate from the private domicile of the official, and, in general, bureaucracy segregates official activity as something distinct from the sphere of private life'. Marx also regarded the public/private division as fundamental to modernity, as we have seen. For Weber there is a symmetrical distinction of the 'personal' and the 'official' in both the 'public' and 'private' spheres, as Marx distinguished these. If within the modern state all 'public monies and equipment are divorced from the private property of the official', then within the modern corporation too 'the executive office is separated from the household, business from private correspondence, and business assets from private fortunes' (1970: 197). This 'separation of business from the household, which completely dominates modern economic life', he maintains elsewhere, is one of two key factors (the other being rational bookkeeping) in whose absence 'the modern rational organization of the capitalistic enterprise would not have been possible' (1974: 21–2). This separation is once again a mainly occidental phenomenon, whose 'beginnings ... are to be found as early as the Middle Ages' (1970: 197).

Here Weber goes some way towards addressing what I argued was a fundamental lacuna in Marx. With the dissolution of agrarian communes and the rise of private property in land, he claims, the household community shrinks to a point where 'the father with his wife and children functions as the unit in property relations'. Along with this go two other major shifts in the character of the modern household: 'its function has become restricted to the field of consumption, and its management placed on an accounting basis' (1966: 94). The present-day household, he says (in 1920), is 'commonly a small family ... based on legitimate marriage considered to be permanent' (1966: 38). Notwithstanding his noting a general tendency towards 'separation between the property of the man and the woman, with a separate accounting' (1966: 94), he is clear that 'today ... all property right vests in the *master* of the house as an individual' (1966: 38). This is one of the distinguishing marks of what in the same text he calls the 'patriarchate' (1966: 52). I have some warrant in the founding fathers, then, for arguing that patriarchy has been a key relation of capitalist production. For a fuller discussion of questions of gender, however, Weber refers us to his wife's work (which, he reassures his readers, is 'in general free of bias'!) (1966: 271).

We might note that recent historical work has established beyond any doubt that such a 'nuclear' household, far from being (as sociologists once commonly presumed) the consequence either of capitalism or industrialization, long preceded both in North West Europe – and, so far as is known, only there. It was part of a singular demographic regime in which both sexes married late and many people remained single, with ensuing limitations on family size and population growth. In general new households were set up on marriage, and marriage was deferred until the partners were in a position economically to do this. Alan Macfarlane (1986, 1987; cf. Levine 1989, Seccombe 1990) has argued, to my mind very persuasively, that this wholly unique North West European 'mode of reproduction' was critical to the development of capitalism in that same part of the world. Among other things it facilitated escape from the 'Malthusian' cycles typical of agrarian societies, allowing savings and productive investment. It dissociated adulthood from parenthood, fostering 'individualism' as a cultural norm, and rendered decisions over when, whether and whom to marry, and how many children to have, matters of economic calculation. Since the labour of grown-up children did not flow back to the parental family, children became an economic cost rather than, as elsewhere, a familial asset. This regime also provided a pool of wage labour in the shape of youthful servants of both sexes, servanthood becoming for most a phase in the life-cycle. Macfarlane relates this distinctive mode of reproduction to other 'peculiarities' of North West European (and above all of English) historical development, notably to the early formation of machineries of state capable of guaranteeing individual property rights at law. I cannot further rehearse what seems to me to be one of the most suggestive of recent challenges to the assumptions of 'classical' sociology (if frequently an overstated one) any more fully here. Suffice it to say that if there is any substance in Macfarlane's contentions, they underline just how critical for capitalism is its infrastructure of familial forms (and therewith, of gender relations).

2

There are obvious affinities between Max Weber's conception of bureaucracy (and in particular of the modern bureaucratic state) and Marx's, discussed earlier. Weber sees 'a developed money economy' as being the 'normal precondition for the unchanged and continued existence ... of pure bureaucratic administrations' – if only because bureaucrats are salaried – and inversely views the rational-bureaucratic state as a *sine qua non* for rational capitalism (1970: 204–5). Like Marx, he argues that it is only in 'the complete depersonalization of administrative management by bureaucracy' that 'the separation of public and private' spheres fundamental to capitalism is realized 'fully and in principle' (1970: 239). Marx would doubtless have approved his observations on the tensions between democracy and bureaucracy. 'Bureaucracy inevitably accompanies modern *mass democracy* in contrast to the democratic self-government of small homogeneous units', and 'the democratization of society in its totality, and in the *modern* sense of the term, whether actual or perhaps merely formal, is an especially favourable basis for bureaucratization'. But, Weber warns, '"democratization", in the sense here intended, does not necessarily mean an increasingly active share of the governed in the authority of the social structure'; 'the most decisive thing here – indeed it is rather exclusively so – is the *levelling of the governed* in opposition to the ruling and bureaucratically articulated group, which in turn may occupy a quite autocratic position, both in fact and in form' (1970: 224–6, 231). As with Marx, the political subjectivity of the governed is illusory, the reality that they are objects of policy and administration. Like Marx too, Weber notes the association of bureaucracy and control of knowledge: 'the official secret', he argues, is 'the specific invention of bureaucracy', and for it 'nothing is so fanatically defended' (1970: 233).

Weber's is, in fact, a severely realistic, if not a cynical, conception of the state: 'a relation of men dominating men, a relation supported by means of legitimate (i.e. considered to be legitimate) violence'. He cites Trotsky's words at Brest-Litovsk – 'every state is founded on force' – in his support. The 'inner justification' of the modern state, differentiating it from its precursors, is 'the belief in the validity of legal statute and functional "competence" based on rationally created *rules*' (1970: 78–9). But it remains the case that 'the modern state is a compulsory association which organizes domination' (1970: 82). To my mind, however, the most significant of Weber's echoes of Marx lie in the contrast both draw between personalized and impersonal modes of administration and forms of power, and the bases of their legitimacy (in Weber's terms, 'traditional' or 'patrimonial' vs. 'rational-legal'). This threads each of their accounts of both capitalism and the modern state (and for both it connects the two).

For Weber

> it is decisive for the specific nature of modern loyalty to an of-
> fice that ... it does not establish loyalty to a *person*, like the vas-
> sal's or disciple's faith in feudal or in patrimonial relations of
> authority. Modern loyalty is devoted to impersonal and func-
> tional purposes.

(1970: 199)

'The "objective" discharge of business primarily means a discharge of business according to *calculable rules* and "without regard for persons"'. He goes on:

> 'without regard for persons' is also the watchword of the mar-
> ket and, in general, of all pursuit of naked economic interests.
> A consistent execution of bureaucratic domination means the
> levelling of status 'honor'. Hence, if the principle of the free
> market is not at the same time restricted, it means the universal
> domination of the 'class situation'.

(1970: 215)

This is exactly the same connection Marx drew between a society
of abstractly equal individuals (who are concretely unequal members of social classes) and the modern 'political' state; and just like
Marx, who counterposed relations based on law and relations
based on privilege, Weber centres the key metaphor of the level
playing field. 'The characteristic principle of bureaucracy', he says,
is

> the abstract regularity of the execution of authority, which is a
> result of the demand for 'equality before the law' in the per-
> sonal and functional sense – hence, of the horror of 'privilege',
> and the principled rejection of doing business 'from case to
> case'.

(1970: 224)

Marx spoke in *Capital* of the 'revolting prerogatives' of feudalism,
and in *The German Ideology* of the need for law within bourgeois
society 'to hold good for everybody' (1867a: 715; 1846a: 329–30).
These themes are writ large in Weber's opposition of 'rational'
law and 'Kadi-justice', in other words justice that works on the *ad*

hoc basis of the perceived merits of the individual case.

'All non-bureaucratic forms of domination', he says, combine 'a sphere of strict traditionalism' and a parallel 'sphere of free arbitrariness and lordly grace' (1970: 217). Rationalized law is, by contrast, characterized by 'the rule of general and abstract norms' (1970: 219). Weber caustically notes that 'the propertyless masses especially are not served by a formal "equality before the law" and a "calculable" adjudication and administration, as demanded by "bourgeois" interests'. The former's demand is always for '*substantive* justice oriented toward some concrete instance and person' (1970: 220–1). All of this is eminently consistent with Marx's view that 'individuals are now ruled by *abstractions*, whereas previously they were dependent on one another' – something I argued was the *Leitmotif* of his account of modernity. Weber comments also upon the complementary idealization of modern forms of communality, as did Marx. 'Ideas such as "state", "church", "community", "party", or "enterprise"', he maintains, 'are thought of as being realized in a community', whereas in reality 'they provide an ideological halo for the master.' They are '*ersatz*' (1970: 199). He remarks 'the sure interests of the bureaucracy for the conditions of maintaining its power' via 'the canonization of the abstract and "objective" idea of "reasons of state"' – an idea, he says, which is 'specifically modern' (1970: 220). But there are major differences between Marx and Weber here too; and in this case they sustain fundamentally opposed evaluations of the future of capitalism.

3

In Max Weber's view, 'the decisive reason for the advance of bureaucratic organization has always been its purely *technical* superiority over any other form of organization'. Extending his recurrent parallel with the capitalist organization of material production, he maintains that bureaucracy 'compares with other organizations exactly as does the machine with the non-mechanical modes of production'. It provides optimal 'precision, speed, unambiguity, knowledge of the files, continuity, discretion, unity, strict subordination, reduction of friction and of material and personal costs', and it does this 'the more the bureaucracy is "de-

"dehumanized", the more completely it succeeds in eliminating from official business love, hatred, and all purely personal, irrational and emotional elements which escape calculation' (1970: 214–16). This formidable efficiency in turn means that 'once it is fully established, bureaucracy is among those social structures which are the hardest to destroy'. Bureaucracy is 'a form of power relation ... that is practically unshatterable'. Unlike those who previously embodied power as 'notables' – courtiers, table companions, and so forth – 'the professional bureaucrat is chained to his activity by his entire material and ideal existence'. Just like Marx's detail worker whose labour-power cannot be exercised except in his master's factory, the bureaucrat 'is only a single cog in an ever-moving mechanism which prescribes to him an essentially fixed route of march'. 'The ruled, for their part, cannot dispense with or replace the bureaucratic apparatus once it exists' either. 'Expert training, a functional specialization of work, and an attitude set for habitual and virtuoso-like mastery of single yet methodically integrated functions' mean that the result of the bureaucracy being disabled will be 'chaos'. Thus bureaucratic 'discipline increasingly becomes the basis of all order'; for 'compliance has been conditioned into the officials ... and the governed' (1970: 228–9).

Rational bureaucracy, in the famous image (earlier used in *The Protestant Ethic* of 'victorious capitalism'), is an 'iron cage' from which escape is ever more improbable. 'Iron cage' is in fact an unfortunate translation (Kent 1983). *The Protestant Ethic* speaks of 'the care for external goods', which Baxter says should 'lie on the shoulders of the "saint like a light cloak, which can be thrown aside at any moment"', turning into *ein stahlhartes Gehäuse*: a casing, or housing, as hard as steel (1974: 181). If we are to translate metaphorically, a better choice of analogy than Bunyan's man in the iron cage (which inspired Talcott Parsons's rendition) might be the shell (also *Gehäuse*) on a snail's back: a burden perhaps, but something impossible to live without, in either sense of the word. A cage remains an external restraint: unlock the door, and one walks out free. This *Gehäuse* is a prison altogether stronger, the armour of modern subjectivity itself. Dependency on 'mechanized petrification' has become an integral part of who we are.

Weber observes that the 'objective indispensability' and '"impersonal"' character of bureaucracy mean that 'the mechanism – in contrast to feudal orders based upon personal piety – is easily made to work for anybody who knows how to gain control over it'. As in Marx, power has become divorced from persons and objectified – intellectualized and disembodied. One example of 'indispensability' Weber gives is interesting, because Marx used it too: 'with all the changes in France since the time of the First Empire, the power machine has remained essentially the same [...] In classic fashion, France has demonstrated how this process [bureaucratization] has substituted *coups d'état* for "revolutions"' (1970: 229–30). In 1871 Marx wrote, of the Paris Commune, that 'all [previous] revolutions perfected the state machinery instead of throwing off this deadening incubus', while the Commune was 'a revolution against the *State* itself' (1871: 484–6). He drew the moral that 'the working class cannot simply lay hold on the ready-made state machinery and wield it for their own purpose' (1871: 548), and repudiated the *Communist Manifesto*'s 'revolutionary measures' for centralization in the hands of the state accordingly (1872). The 'machine' as such needed to be smashed. Weber was more pessimistic. As the 'objective indispensability' of modernity's bureaucratic forms of social organization – including those of private capital – grows, 'the idea of eliminating these organizations becomes more and more utopian'. Quite simply, for him 'such a machine makes "revolution", in the sense of the forcible creation of entirely new formations of authority, technically more and more impossible, especially when the apparatus controls the modern means of communication ... and also by virtue of its internal rationalized structure' (1970: 230).

Weber's hostility to socialism must be understood in this context. In the political sphere 'the great state and the mass party are the classic soil for bureaucratization' (1970: 209), and socialism elevates both, just as, in the economic realm, the socialization of the means of production would, he believed, merely increase the power of bureaucratized management. 'In any rationally organized socialistic economy', he wrote in *Economy and Society*, 'the expropriation of all the workers would be retained and merely brought to completion by the expropriation of private owners' (1964: 248). His essay on socialism of 1916 takes the view that 'it is the dictatorship of the official, not that of the worker, which ... is on the advance', and ends with the question: 'Who would then take control of and direct this new economy? On this point the Communist Manifesto is silent' (1978b: 260, 262). Weber follows in the footsteps of Tönnies and Simmel in concluding that a rational socialism would be a 'house of servitude', the perfection, not at all the negation, of Marx's 'severance'. Writing in 1918, he observes of Russia that

> the Soviets have preserved, or rather reintroduced, the highly paid enterpriser, the group wage, the Taylor system, military and workshop discipline, and a search for foreign capital. Hence, in a word, the Soviets have had to accept again absolutely *all* the things that Bolshevism has been fighting as class institutions. They have had to do so in order to keep the state and the economy going at all.

He comments too on the revival of the Tsarist secret police as the 'main instrument of [Bolshevik] state power' (1970: 100), and grimly notes the cannibalism of revolutions: 'the materialist interpretation of history is no cab to be taken at will; it does not stop short of the promoters of revolutions'. 'Emotional revolutionalism' is succeeded by 'the traditionalist routine of everyday life', and 'the faith becomes part of the conventional phraseology of political Philistines and banausic technicians'. Sustaining revolutionary power involves thorough 'depersonalization and routinization, in short ... [a] psychic proletarianization, in the interests of discipline', and 'the following of a crusader usually degenerates ... into a quite common stratum of spoilsmen' (1970: 125).

I am quoting these words in the wake of what I hope will be celebrated as the 1989 Revolution in Eastern Europe. Millions, who have experienced its fruits, would appear to endorse Weber's judgement on what has masqueraded as 'socialism' in this century. The 'spoilsmen', we now know, have been salting away billions, stolen through their command over what Marx would have called the surplus labour of their people, in numbered Swiss bank accounts. I think enough time has passed to suggest that such 'perversions' cannot adequately be analysed merely in terms of 'betrayal' by individuals. The possibility needs to be faced, even by those persuaded of the validity of Marx's indictment of capitalism, that something may be awry in the very idea of socialism itself.

Marx described property, for him the 'hidden secret' of all social structures, as 'the power of disposing of the labour-power of others', and warned that it could not be defined abstractly but only through the exposition of a given set of social relations of production (1846a: 46; 1847: 197). Arguably socialism is the epitome of such power, concentrating it entirely in the hands of that *Stand* who identify themselves with and as 'the state', and the form taken by socialist production relations hitherto has been the command of this 'machine'. Given this kind of economic structure, there is every good *Marxist* reason to expect a routinized tyranny of rule by the *nomenklatura* and, through time, of privileged clans within it. The onus, I think, is on socialists to demonstrate that this need not be so. Marx's refusal to write recipes for the 'cookshops of the future' cannot forever provide the excuse for evading the ethical and intellectual questions raised by what is now three quarters of a century of a corrupt, unproductive and exceedingly bloody past. Nor should a ritual invocation of the undoubted inequities (and systematic corruptions) of capitalism any longer be thought sufficient justification of what, on the evidence, is scant alternative. Invidious as capitalism might be, the moral superiority of socialism can no longer be presumed *a priori*. An ethic of responsibility (as Weber called it) requires attention not simply to the beauty of ends, but equally to the consequences of the empirical means that can conceivably be used to attain them.

Weber, I imagine, would not have been overly surprised by the fate of socialism in the twentieth century; although the relative ease with which, in the end, apparently monolithic regimes have crumbled across Europe ought perhaps to lead us to question his thesis of bureaucracy's essential unshatterability. Power is a more complex relation than he allows: if, as I have suggested, it resides finally in the regulation of subjectivities, then it is always vulnerable to the untruthfulness of those representations as argued by Marx. Time and again the best paradigm for its analysis turns out to be Hans Andersen's cautionary tale of the Emperor's new clothes. Weber himself, however, drew the supremely ironic conclusion that it is now above all capitalism itself, that vehicle of rationalization *par excellence*, whose continued survival alone prevents a monocratic bureaucratization of the whole of social life. And, he believed, this capitalism might not endure. It is unlikely to be succeeded by a New Jerusalem. Rather,

> in all probability someday the bureaucratization of society will encompass capitalism too, just as it did in Antiquity. We too will then enjoy the benefits of bureaucratic 'order' instead of the 'anarchy' of free enterprise, and this order will be essentially the same as that which characterized the Roman Empire and – even more – the New Empire in Egypt and the Ptolemaic state.

> (1983: 159)

4

More is at stake here than simply a critique of modern socialism. Weber's antipathy is rooted in a much deeper disenchantment with rationalization itself. Though an acute observer of modernity, he was, as David Frisby puts it, 'a determined anti-modernist' (1985: 2). It is no accident that in his wrenching *cri de coeur* 'Science as a vocation' – perhaps the most profound reflection on the modern condition to be found anywhere in his work – Weber recalls both Nietzsche and Baudelaire. This was an address that he delivered at Munich University in the year 1918, when the savagery which lurks at the heart of civilization was in full flood. It cannot have much comforted his audience. 'Since Nietzsche', he says, 'we realize that something can be beautiful, not only in spite of the aspect in which it is not good, but rather in that very aspect. You will find this expressed earlier in the *Fleurs du mal*' (1970: 148). It is not a question here of either/or, but rather of both/and; of intractable paradoxes, not contradictions resolvable by Hegelian sleight of hand. Modern life has this quality. It is like the well-known drawing which can be seen at once as a beautiful young woman and as an old and ugly crone. Rational, scientific, intellectual 'disenchantment of the world' implies not only an emancipation from magic and superstition, but also an irretrievable loss. In Weber's hands, this realization amounts to very much more than a conventional conservative nostalgia for an idealized past.

Let me for a last time contrast Weber and Marx. Writing in Paris, the 'capital of the nineteenth century', at the start of 1844 – in the same essay in which he 'discovered' the proletariat as the 'material weapon' of philosophy – Marx asserted that 'criticism of religion is the beginning of all criticism'. Religion, as his famous cadences have it, is 'the sigh of the oppressed creature, the heart of a heartless world ... the spirit of spiritless conditions. It is the *opium of the people*'; and 'to abolish religion as the *illusory* happiness of the people is to demand their *real* happiness'. Disillusionment – and reason – are here unambiguously positive, 'progressive'. 'Criticism has torn up the imaginary flowers from the chain not so that man shall wear the unadorned, bleak chain but so that he will shake off the chain and pluck the living flower.' The criticism of religion 'disillusions man to make him think and act and shape his reality like a man who has been disillusioned and has come to reason, so that he will revolve around himself' (1843d: 175–6). Weber had a darker view of the matter. Disillusion meant disenchantment, in both senses of the word; and 'reason' lay at the very root of the problem.

For Weber, to espouse religion, in a world overwhelmed by the rationality of science, was no more possible than for Marx. He voiced compassion for those who, unable 'to bear the fate of the times', fled into the arms of the church; but he regarded this as involving an 'intellectual sacrifice' (1970: 155). As he bluntly put it, 'redemption from the rationalism and intellectualism of science is the fundamental presupposition of living in unity with the divine' (1970: 142). Science – and a world built on the principles of scientific rationality – must inexorably corrode religion, except as a vehicle of mystical escape from rationalism itself. Weber was not prepared to sacrifice his intellect. He declares a vocation for science, and affirms its value (for those *few* who dare to pursue it). But he does so in a way that totally lacks Marx's rationalist (and modernist) stridency, and is itself paradoxical. Weber affirms science, he says, 'from precisely the standpoint that hates intellectualism as the worst devil'. It is in order 'to settle with this devil ... to see the devil's ways to the end in order to realize his power and his limitations' and 'not take to flight before him as so many do nowadays' (1970: 152) that he endorses the value of science, and, furthermore, of a science which is 'ethically neutral'. The latter prescription is often misunderstood, not to say turned on its head. Far from being a demand for technocratic neutrality, it was an attempt to protect the sphere of free value judgement from the pretensions of scientific imperialism. 'An *attitude of moral indifference*', he is adamant, 'has no connection with *scientific* "objectivity"' (1949: 60). Weber regards scientific rationality as the most efficient technical means of understanding the world, including the 'devil' of rationalization itself – but that is all. He is very well aware of the ironies of this position.

Science has *no* meaning that transcends 'the purely practical and technical'. The 'former illusions' that it might be the 'way to true being' (the Greeks), the 'way to true art' and thereby the 'way to true nature' (the Renaissance), the 'way to true God' (Protestantism) or – a modernist fallacy, nowadays believed in only by 'a few big children in university chairs' – the 'way to true happiness', have been dispelled (1970: 139–43). Science is a means of establishing the facts of the case, no more and no less. And between the realm of facts and the realm of values there is a 'logical gulf' (1949: 51–63). Science (Weber quotes Tolstoy) 'is meaningless because it gives no answer to our question, the only question important for us: "What shall we do and how shall we live?"' (1970: 143). At best science may provide empirical knowledge individuals might take into account in determining the practical means of attaining or consequences of striving for particular ends; and it may thereby serve those who choose to live by an 'ethic of responsibility' rather than an 'absolute ethic' of ultimate ends (1970: 118f.). It need not: the trains to Treblinka doubtless ran on time. But science cannot provide or evaluate ends themselves. We cannot '"refute scientifically" the ethic of the Sermon on the Mount' (1970: 148). Science, in short, has *nothing* to say on questions of value, or in other words, so far as Weber is concerned, is silent on exactly that which gives all human life and action their meaning.

Worse still, science, in its very rationality, undermines exactly those standpoints from which value is capable of being derived: above all religious ethics. Empirically, science and technology demonstrate that 'there are no mysterious incalculable forces that come into play ... one can, in principle, master all things by calculation' (1970: 139). Logically, reason shows the foundations of all values – including those of science itself – to be arbitrary. It is the lone individual who 'has to decide which is God for him and which is the devil' (1970: 148). This predicament is not an easy one; for not only are transcendental bases of decision no longer available, there can be no rational criteria for choosing between ultimate ends either. That which alone gives to human lives their point and purpose thus becomes, in a thoroughly rationalized world, irremediably contingent – and transitory, and fugitive. In fine, rational disenchantment not only destroys the possibility of that kind of religious framework which can bestow transcendental meaning on everyday actions, but it is incapable in principle of furnishing any kind of substitute for it. This is what I mean by irretrievable loss. There can be no going back – such contingency is the modern condition. To be disillusioned, *pace* Marx, is to 'wear the bleak, unadorned chain'. There are no living flowers waiting to be plucked, unless it be Baudelaire's *fleurs du mal*.

Yet still we must live, as did the ancients: and the stark question, 'Which of the warring gods shall we serve?' (1970: 155), far from going away, takes on new urgency. 'Our civilization destines us to realize more clearly these struggles again, after our eyes have been blinded for a thousand years' by 'the grandiose moral fervour of Christian ethics'. And today 'many old gods ascend from their graves; they are disenchanted and hence take the form of impersonal forces. They strive to gain power over our lives and again they resume their eternal struggle with one another'. It is, Weber says, 'how to measure up to *workaday* existence' in this disenchanted world that is so 'hard for modern man' (1970: 149). His personal answer is the ethic of responsibility, which he explains with eloquence in 'Politics as a vocation'. Its essence is that 'one has to give an account of the foreseeable results of one's action' (1970: 120). His social prognosis is not a cheerful one. 'Not summer's bloom lies ahead of us, but rather a polar night of icy darkness and hardness, no matter which group may triumph externally now. Where there is nothing, not only the Kaiser but the proletarian has lost his rights' (1970: 128).

Humanity, and humaneness, are everywhere in retreat before these impersonal deities of modernity. Though Weber does not

say so, *L'Être Suprême* – Reason – who presided over the guillotine in the Year One of the modern age heralded much. For him,
'the ultimate and most sublime values have retreated from public
life either into the transcendental realm of mystic life or into the
brotherliness of direct and personal human relations'. 'Today', it
is 'only within the smallest and intimate circles, in personal human
situations, in *pianissimo*, that something is pulsating that corresponds to the prophetic *pneuma*, which in former times swept
though the great communities like a firebrand, welding them
together'. Humane values are hemmed into that little world of
Penn's letters. The wider society is a mechanism without a soul,
and the individuals within it become prey to *ersatz* religion and
'academic prophecies' of a sort capable of producing 'fanatical
sects but never a genuine community' (1970: 155). These words
were written in the land of Goethe, Schiller and Beethoven, just
fifteen years before Hitler took power. What modernity leaves us
with is the unprecedented loneliness of the single individual, in
the face, now, of no god at all, and the passing consolation of personal integrity. It is 'a godless and prophetless time' – and a peri-
lous one (1970: 153).

Once the imaginary flowers have been swept away – less by
'criticism' than the wholesale rationalization of life itself – 'man'
indeed has no choice but to 'revolve around himself'. Or herself,
since we are talking of real, not abstract individuals. But central to
that self is what the novelist Milan Kundera, who also draws on
Nietzsche, calls the unbearable lightness of being. Where all
values become equivalent, 'everything is pardoned in advance and
therefore everything cynically permitted'. Even the guillotine is
bathed in the aura of nostalgia, its bloodiness 'turned into mere
words, theories, discussions ... lighter than feathers, frightening no
one'. As an exile from that faraway country which (as his com-
patriot Josef Škvorecký reminds us) has been blessed, during the
last seventy years, with every political system known to modernity,
Kundera surely speaks from a relevant experience. He sees this
'profound moral perversity' as implicit in 'the non-existence of return'. Since events do not eternally recur, their substance is lost
and their horror is mitigated (1985: 3–4). From Marx onward, this
lack of recurrence is what has been claimed as the distinctive fea-

ture of modernity. And this is exactly where Weber leaves us, expressing a peculiarly modern disenchantment:

> for civilized man death has no meaning. It has none because the individual life of civilized man, placed into an infinite 'progress', according to its own imminent meaning should never come to an end; for there is always a further step ahead of one who stands in the march of progress. And no man who comes to die stands upon the peak which lies in infinity. Abraham, or some peasant of the past, died 'old and satiated with life' because he stood in the organic cycle of life; because his life, in terms of its meaning and on the eve of his days, had given to him what life had to offer; because for him there remained no puzzles he might wish to solve; and therefore he could have had enough of life. Whereas civilized man, placed in the midst of the continuous enrichment of culture by ideas, knowledge, and problems, may become 'tired of life' but not 'satiated with life'. He catches only the most minute part of what the life of the spirit brings forth ever anew, and what he seizes is always something provisional and not definitive, and therefore death for him is a meaningless occurrence. And because death is meaningless, civilized life as such is meaningless; by its very 'progressiveness' it gives death the imprint of meaninglessness (1970: 139–40).

We return to *le transitoire, le fugitif, le contingent*. As the sea of faith withdraws, we are left, alone, on the naked shingles of the world. It is a bleak vision, but one, I think, impossible to ignore in the century of Passchendaele, Auschwitz and Pol Pot. This is indeed a world of *mors immortalis*.

5

An elective affinity, then, for the modern age: between those qualities we most prize in scientific discourse – objectivity, universality, logic, consistency, simplicity, systematicity, quantifiability, precision, unambiguity and a certain aesthetic elegance – and the principles upon which Weber's (and Marx's) machines of modernity operate. In neither is there room for the concrete, the particular, and the personal. These are banished to the 'irrational' realm of 'private life'. The modern era, as Marx said, is ruled by abstractions. It may be that capitalism is the foundation upon which this rule is first erected; Marx and Weber provide compelling reason for thinking it is. But it may also be that today, this abstraction has gone very far beyond capitalism itself, and we will not be rid of it just by changing the title deeds on property (or still less by 'capturing' 'state power'). This is the enduring importance of Weber's analysis of rationalization and the bureaucratization which is its ubiquitous concomitant. Disembodied, the very forms of our sociality turn against us, and within them there is no place for humane values. The soulful corporation or the compassionate state are, by virtue of the very constitution of these social forms, contradictions in terms. This was also, of course, the message of Marx's critique of alienation. But Weber, I think, quite legitimately extends Marx's argument, to a point where capitalism, because of the selfsame 'anarchy' that grounds this alienation, appears now as the ironic guarantor that the 'iron casing' of a new Ptolemaic order does not imprison all. Insubstantial as modern bourgeois liberties may be – and Weber had few illusions on the matter – they are preferable to none at all. The 'private life' of the 'abstract individual' becomes the pathetic sanctuary of humanity.

This makes any notion of an emancipatory politics deeply problematic, in so far as the very forms in which modern politics are conducted – states, parties, ideologies – partake of the same nexus of estrangement. The history of socialism, in this century, has confirmed Weber's worst forebodings; its proponents have proved all too willing to strike Faustian bargains with his modern devils, notably the machines of industry and state. I do not draw the conclusion that improvement of the human condition is impossible; but I would insist that it is no longer capitalism alone, but the monstrously abstracted progeny it has engendered, that is our problem. The modern world is in one respect at least different from all of its predecessors. Only now is the survival of the human race itself in jeopardy. What earlier century had even a presentiment that such destructive forces slumbered in the lap of social labour?

The ultimate measure of the awesome power, and the fundamental violence, of unfettered abstraction is to be found in the millions upon millions of nameless corpses which this most vicious of centuries has left as its memorial, human sacrifices to one or another of Weber's renascent modern gods. War itself is not new; modernity's contribution is to have waged it, with characteristic efficiency, under the sign of various totalizing abstractions which name and claim the lives of all. Here the 'lightness' of the modern subject becomes all too evident, and the truth of the real living individual as Marx's 'plaything of alien forces' is written in blood. These abstractions, I should perhaps add, have by no means only been socialist: there were killing fields in Cambodia before what the Khmer Rouge, following Robespierre's precedent, proclaimed as Year One. But nor can they plausibly all be laid at the door of capitalism. The nineteenth century, when things might reasonably have appeared so, is long over. We are at another *fin de siècle*.

In *The German Ideology* of 1845–6, Marx asked himself a question:

Individuals always proceeded, and always proceed, from themselves. Their relations are the relations of their real life-process. How does it happen that their relations assume an independent existence over against them? and that the forces of their own life become superior to them?

(1846a: 93)

Capitalism is a vital part of the answer, for reasons explored in this book. It is the ground upon which other modern forms of estrangement arose, and furnishes the template for the 'severance' which gives modernity's machines their terrible force. But it is this wider mechanization of human social life itself which is the problem, and this is no longer, if it ever was, confined to those theatres within which capital rules. Mechanization is of course but a metaphor. What we are actually talking of are our own forms of sociality and subjectivity, as Karl Marx was among the first to make clear. Weber's devils stare out of Baudelaire's mirror.

I do not wholly share Weber's pessimism: it may be that out of this 'mechanical petrification ... new prophets will arise, or there will be a great rebirth of old ideas and ideals' (1974: 182). But I believe it should be taken seriously; and most of all by those who do aspire not merely to interpret the world, but to change it.

Suggestions for further reading

Marx and Weber each wrote an enormous amount, and the secondary literature on both is vast. So are works on both capitalism and modernity. Here I merely indicate some ways into this literature for the student. More detailed references on the sources used in this book may be found in the Bibliography.

(1) Marx

An accessible anthology, oriented towards Marx's sociology and arranged thematically, is D. Sayer (ed.) *Readings from Karl Marx* (1989) in the Routledge 'Key Texts' series. For a more extensive and generally representative selection D. McLellan (ed.) *Selected Writings* (Oxford 1977) or E. Kamenka (ed.) *The Portable Marx* (Harmondsworth 1983) are both very good value. *Readings from Karl Marx* contains an extensive and up-to-date bibliography of Marx's own writings, collections and anthologies, and secondary literature. Of modern secondary discussions covering the aspects of Marx's theory discussed in this book, I would particularly recommend Bertell Ollman's *Alienation: Marx's critique of man in capitalist society* (1976), despite the difficulty of its opening chapter. A fuller exposition of the view of Marx taken here may be found in my book *The violence of abstraction* (Sayer 1987). David McLellan's *Karl Marx: his life and thought* (1973) is probably the most scholarly biography, and does a good job of putting Marx in his historical and intellectual context. It is also readable.

(2) Weber

The best all-round anthology of Weber, a superb introduction, remains H. Gerth and C. Wright Mills *From Max Weber* (Weber 1970). Also useful is Andreski's more focused collection *On capitalism, bureaucracy and religion* (Weber 1983). Of longer studies, *The Protestant Ethic* is obviously critical to Weber's views on capitalism; but it should be supplemented by a reading of Part 4 of the *General Economic History*, together with the essay on 'The Protestant sects' in *From Max Weber*. Peter Lassmann and Irving Velody (1988) have done the world a service with their new edition of Weber's 'Science as a vocation', a text central to understanding his position on modernity. Karl Lowith's classic essay *Max Weber and Karl Marx* (Lowith 1982) remains unsurpassed, to my mind, as an account of what Weber understood by 'rationalization', and the many affinities between his views and Marx's. W. Mommsen and J. Osterhammel (eds) *Max Weber and his contemporaries* is thorough on context (1987); Marianne Weber's biography of her husband (1975) is also invaluable. Of standard general introductions to Weber's thought, Bendix (1962) or Freund (1969) remain useful; an excellent recent study is Kasler (1988). Other recent works on Weber which take up the issues addressed in this book include Brubaker (1984), Collins (1986), Hennis (1988), Holton and Turner (1989), Schluchter (1981), Tribe (1989), Turner (1981) and Whimster and Lash (1987). A recent collection on 'the Marx–Weber debate' is Wiley (1987).

(3) Capitalism and Modernity

On the historiography of capitalism, an issue not discussed here, between them Hilton (1978), Aston and Philpin (1985), Braudel (1977), Macfarlane (1987) and Baechler, Hall and Mann (1988) give a plentiful introduction to recent debates. This book has only considered the issue of modernity in Marx and Weber themselves. For a broader perspective see the works by Berman, Frisby and Harvey listed in the Bibliography. I would also suggest, as a strong antidote to the 'occidentalist' assumptions common to Marxist and Weberian sociologies of 'the' 'modern' 'world', a reading of two iconoclastic contemporary classics: Said's *Orientalism* (1979) and Bernal's *Black Athena* (1987). For a feminist critique of the masculinity of classical sociological constructions of modernity, see R. Sydie *Natural women, cultured men* (1987). For myself, I think the essence of much of what social theories of modernity try to grasp in a different idiom is captured remarkably in two novels: Milan Kundera's *The unbearable lightness of being*, and Joseph Škvorecký's *Engineer of human souls*. Fittingly, both are emigré literature.

Bibliography

Abercrombie, N., Hill, S. and Turner, B. S. (1986). *Sovereign individuals of capitalism*. London, Allen and Unwin.

Abrams, P. (1988) 'Notes on the difficulty of studying the state'. *Journal of Historical Sociology*, 1(1).

Anderson, B. (1983) *Imagined communities*. London, Verso.

Ariès, P. (1962) *Centuries of childhood*. New York, Vintage.

Arnold, M. (1967) *Poetry and prose*. (ed.) J. Bryson. London, Rupert Hart-Davis.

Aston, T. and Philpin, C. (eds) (1985) *The Brenner debate*. Cambridge University Press.

Baechler, J., Hall, J. A. and Mann, M. (eds) (1988) *Europe and the rise of capitalism*. Oxford and New York, Basil Blackwell.

Baudelaire, C. (1970) *Paris spleen*. New York, New Directions.

Baudelaire, C. (1986) *My heart laid bare and other prose writings*. London, Soho.

Bendix, R. (1962) *Max Weber: an intellectual portrait*. New York, Doubleday Anchor.

Berman, M. (1982) *All that is solid melts into air: the experience of modernity*. New York, Simon and Schuster.

Bernal, M. (1987) *Black Athena: the Afroasiatic roots of classical civilization*. New Brunswick, NJ, Rutgers University Press.

Braudel, F. (1977) *Afterthoughts on material civilization and capitalism*. Baltimore, Johns Hopkins University Press.

Braudel, F. (1978) *Civilization and capitalism*, 3 vols. London, Fontana.

Braverman, H. (1974) *Labor and monopoly capital*. New York, Monthly Review Press.

Brubaker, R. (1984) *The limits of rationality: an essay on the social and moral thought of Max Weber*. London, Allen and Unwin.

Campbell, C. (1987) *The romantic ethic and the spirit of modern consumerism*. Oxford and New York, Basil Blackwell.

Collins, R. (1986) *Weberian social theory*. Cambridge University Press.

Corrigan, P. (1977) 'Feudal relics or capitalist monuments: notes on the sociology of unfree labour'. *Sociology*, 11.

Corrigan, P. (1990) *Social forms/human capacities: essays in authority and difference*. London, Routledge.

Corrigan, P. and Sayer, D. (1985) *The great arch: English state formation as cultural revolution*. Oxford and New York, Basil Blackwell.

Corrigan, P. and Sayer, D. (forthcoming) 'From the body politic to the national interest: English state formation in comparative and historical perspective'. Forthcoming in N. Dirks (ed.) *Culture and colonialism*, Princeton University Press.

Denis, C. (1989) 'The genesis of American capitalism: an historical inquiry into state theory'. *Journal of Historical Sociology*, 2(4).

Donne, J. (1975) *Selected poems*. Harmondsworth, Penguin.

Durkheim, E. (1957) *Professional ethics and civic morals*. London, Routledge.

Durkheim, E. (1973) *On morality and society*, (ed.) R. N. Bellah. Chicago University Press.

Durkheim, E. (1976) *Elementary forms of the religious life*. London, Allen and Unwin.

Durkheim, E. (1984) *The division of labour in society*. London, Macmillan.

Elias, N. (1982) *The civilizing process*, 2 vols. Oxford and New York, Basil Blackwell.

Foucault, M. (1977) *Discipline and punish: the birth of the prison*. London, Allen Lane.

Foucault, M. (1980) *The history of sexuality*. Vol. 1. New York, Vintage.

Foucault, M. (1982) 'The subject and power'. *Critical Inquiry*, 8.

Foucault, M. (1988) 'Technologies of the self'. In L. H. Martin, H. Gutman and P. H. Hutton (eds) *Technologies of the self, a seminar with Michel Foucault*. London, Tavistock.

Freund, J. (1969) *The sociology of Max Weber*. New York, Vintage.

Frisby, D. (1985) *Fragments of modernity*. Cambridge, Polity.

Giddens, A. (1981) *A contemporary critique of historical materialism*. Berkeley, University of California Press.

Godelier, M. (1984) *L'idéel et le materiel*. Paris, Fayard.

Harvey, D. (1989) *The condition of postmodernity*. Oxford and New York, Basil Blackwell.

Havel, V. (1989) [Untitled] speech in acceptance of a German peace prize, October 1989. London, *The Independent*, Weekend section, 9 December.

Hennis, W. (1988) *Max Weber: essays in reconstruction*. London, Allen and Unwin.

Hill, C. (1961) 'Protestantism and the rise of capitalism'. In his *Change and continuity in 17th century England*. London, Weidenfeld and Nicolson, 1974.

Hill, C. (1964) *Society and Puritanism in pre-revolutionary England*. London, Secker and Warburg.

Hilton, R. (ed.) (1978) *The transition from feudalism to capitalism*. London, Verso.

Holton, R. and Turner, B. S. (1989) *Max Weber on economy and society*. London, Routledge.

Kasler, D. (1988) *Max Weber*. Cambridge, Polity.

Kelly-Gadol, J. (1977) 'Did women have a Renaissance?' In R. Bridenthal and C. Koonz (eds) *Becoming visible: women in European history*. Boston, Houghton Mifflin.

Kent, S. (1983) 'Weber, Goethe, and the Nietzschean allusion: capturing the source of the "iron cage" metaphor'. *Sociological Analysis*, 44(4).

Kundera, M. (1985) *The unbearable lightness of being*. New York, Harper and Row.

Larner, C. (1981) *Enemies of God: the witch-hunt in Scotland*. London, Chatto and Windus.

Larner, C. (1982) *The thinking peasant: popular and educated belief in pre-industrial culture* (University of Glasgow, Gifford Lectures). Glasgow, Pressgang.

Laslett, P. (1973) *The world we have lost* (2nd edn). London, Methuen.

Lassmann, P. Velody, I. with Martins, H. (1988) *Max Weber's Science as a vocation*. London, Unwin Hyman.

Lenin, V. I. (1902) What is to be done? *Collected Works*, Moscow, Progress, vol. 5.

Levine, D. (1989) 'Recombinant family formation strategies'. *Journal of Historical Sociology*, 2(2).

Linebaugh, P. and Rediker, M. (1990) 'The many-headed hydra: sailors, slaves, and the Atlantic working class in the 18th century'. *Journal of Historical Sociology*, 3(3).

Löwith, K. (1982) *Max Weber and Karl Marx*. London, Allen and Unwin.

Macfarlane, A. (1986) *Marriage and love in England 1300–1840*. Oxford and New York, Basil Blackwell.

Macfarlane, A. (1987) *The culture of capitalism*. Oxford and New York, Basil Blackwell.

McLellan, D. (1973) *Karl Marx: his life and thought*. London, Macmillan.

Macpherson, C. B. (1962) *The political theory of possessive individualism*. Oxford University Press.

Marx, K. and Engels, F. *Collected Works*. London, Lawrence and Wishart, Moscow, Progress, and New York, International, 1975 onward. Cited as CW plus volume number.

Marx, K. (1843a) Contribution to the critique of Hegel's philosophy of law. CW 3.

Marx, K. (1843b) 'On the Jewish question'. CW 3.

Marx, K. (1843c) 'Justification of the correspondent from the Mosel'. CW 1.

Marx, K. (1843d) 'Contribution to the critique of Hegel's philosophy of law: introduction'. CW 3.

Marx, K. (1844) Economic and philosophic manuscripts. CW 3.

Marx, K. (1845) Draft of an article on Friedrich List. CW 4.

Marx, K. (1846a) The German ideology. With F. Engels, CW 5.

Marx, K. (1846b) Letter to Annenkov, 28 December. CW 38.

Marx, K. (1847) The poverty of philosophy. CW 6.

Marx, K. (1848) The manifesto of the communist party. With F. Engels, CW 6.

Marx, K. (1852) The eighteenth Brumaire of Louis Bonaparte. CW 11.

Marx, K. (1853a) 'The British rule in India'. CW 12.

Marx, K. (1853b) 'Future results of the British rule in India'. CW 12.

Marx, K. (1854) Letter to the Labour Parliament. CW 13.

Marx, K. (1855a) 'The British constitution'. CW 14.

Marx, K. (1855b) 'The Association for Administrative Reform. – Peoples' Charter'. CW 14.

Marx, K. (1856) Speech at the anniversary of the *People's Paper*. CW 14.

Marx, K. (1857) General Introduction to the *Grundrisse*. CW 28.

Marx, K. (1858) *Grundrisse*. CW 28. *Idem*, Nicolaus (ed.) *Grundrisse*. Harmondsworth, Penguin, 1973.

Marx, K. (1859) Preface to *A contribution to the critique of political economy*, London, Lawrence and Wishart, 1971.

Marx, K. (1861) 'The crisis in England'. CW 19.

Marx, K. (1863) *Theories of surplus value*, 3 vols. Moscow, Progress, 1963, 1968, 1971.

Marx, K. (1865a) *Capital*, vol. 3. Moscow, Progress, 1971.

Marx, K. (1865b) Value, price and profit. CW 20.

Marx, K. (1866) 'Results of the immediate process of production'. In *Capital*, vol. 1, Harmondsworth, Penguin, 1976.

Marx, K. (1867a) *Capital*, vol. 1. London. Lawrence and Wishart, 1967.

Marx, K. (1867b) Outline of a report on the Irish Question. In *Ireland and the Irish question*. Moscow, Progress, 1968.

Marx, K. (1868a) Letter to L. Kugelmann, 11 July. *Selected correspondence*. Moscow, Progress, 1975.

Marx, K. (1868b) Letter to F. Engels, 8 January. In *Selected correspondence*. Moscow, Progress, 1975.

Marx, K. (1871) *The civil war in France* (text and drafts). CW 22.

Marx, K. (1872) Preface to 1872 German edition of the Communist Manifesto. With F. Engels. In A. J. P. Taylor (ed.) *The Communist Manifesto*. Harmondsworth, Penguin, 1967.

Marx, K. (1877) Letter to editors of *Otechestvenniye Zapiski*. In Shanin 1984.

Marx, K. (1878) *Capital*, vol. 2. Moscow, Progress, 1967.

Marx, K. (1879) Letter to N. Danielson, 10 April. In *Selected correspondence*. Moscow, Progress, 1975.

Marx, K. (1880) Notes on Adolph Wagner. In T. Carver (ed.) *Texts on method*. Oxford, Blackwell, 1974.

Marx, K. (1881a) *Ethnological notebooks*. Assen, Van Gorcum, 1972.

Marx, K. (1881b) Marx–Vasulich correspondence. In Shanin 1984.

Milton, J. (1805) *Paradise lost*. Edinburgh, P. Cairns.

Mommsen, W. (1977) 'Max Weber as a critic of Marxism'. *Canadian Journal of Sociology*, 2(4).

Mommsen, W. and Osterhammel, J. (eds) (1987) *Max Weber and his contemporaries*. London, Allen and Unwin.

Ollman, B. (1976) *Alienation: Marx's critique of man in capitalist society*. Cambridge University Press.

Pinchbeck, I. (1981) *Women workers and the industrial revolution 1750–1850*. London, Virago.

Said, E. (1979) *Orientalism*. New York, Vintage.

Sayer, D. (1983) *Marx's method*, 2nd edn. Brighton, Harvester and Atlantic Highlands, Humanities.

Sayer, D. (1987) *The violence of abstraction: analytic foundations of historical materialism*. London and New York, Basil Blackwell.

Sayer, D. (ed.) (1989) *Readings from Karl Marx*. London and New York, Routledge.

Sayer, D. (1990) 'Reinventing the wheel: Anthony Giddens, Karl Marx, and social change'. In J. Clark, S. and C. Mogdil (eds) *Anthony Giddens: consensus and controversy*. Lewes, Falmer Press.

Schluchter, W. (1981) *The rise of western rationalism*. Berkeley, University of California Press.

Seccombe, W. (1990) 'The western European marriage pattern in historical perspective'. *Journal of Historical Sociology* 3(1).

Seligman, A. (1990) 'Moral authority and Reformation religion: on charisma and the origins of modernity'. Unpublished paper.

Shanin, T. (1984) (ed.) *Late Marx and the Russian road*. London, Routledge.

Simmel, G. (1959) *Sociology of religion*. New York, Wisdom Library.

Simmel, G. (1968) *The conflict in modern culture and other essays*. K. Etzkorn (ed.). New York, Teachers College Press.

Simmel, G. (1978) *The philosophy of money*. London, Routledge.

Škvorecký, J. (1984) 'Failed saxophonist'. *Granta*, 14.

Škvorecký, J. (1986) *The engineer of human souls*. London, Pan.

Sydie, R. (1987) *Natural women, cultured men*. Toronto, Methuen.

Tawney, R. (1938) *Religion and the rise of capitalism*. Harmondsworth, Penguin.

Thomas, K. (1978) *Religion and the decline of magic*. Harmondsworth, Penguin.

Thompson, E. P. (1965) 'Peculiarities of the English'. In his *The poverty of theory and other essays*. London, Merlin, 1978.

Thompson, E. P. (1967) 'Time, work-discipline, and industrial capitalism'. *Past and Present*, 38.

Thompson, E. P. (1968) *The making of the English working class*. Harmondsworth, Penguin.

Thompson, E. P. (1978) 'Eighteenth century English society'. *Social History*, 3.

Tribe, K. (1989) *Reading Weber*. London, Routledge.

Turner, B. S. (1981) *For Weber: essays in the sociology of fate*. London, Routledge and Kegan Paul.

Turner, B. S. (1988) 'Religion and state formation: a commentary upon recent debates'. *Journal of Historical Sociology*, 1(3).

Veblen, T. (1899) *The theory of the leisure class*. New York, Macmillan.

Veyne, P. (ed.) (1987) *A history of private life*. Volume 1, 'From pagan Rome to Byzantium'. Cambridge, Belknap Press of Harvard University Press.

Wallerstein, I. (1974) *The modern world system*, Volume 1. New York, Academic Press.

Weber, Marianne (1975) *Max Weber: a biography*. New York, Wiley.

Weber, M. (1949) *The methodology of the social sciences*. New York, Free Press.

Weber, M. (1964) *The theory of social and economic organization*. New York, Free Press.

Weber, M. (1966) *General economic history*. [Compiled by S. Hellman and M. Palyi from his students' notes from his 1919–20 lectures 'Outlines of Universal Social and Economic History'.] New York, Collier.

Weber, M. (1968) *On charisma and institution building*. S. Eisenstadt (ed.). Chicago University Press.

Weber, M. (1970) *From Max Weber*. H. Gerth and C. Wright Mills (eds). London, Routledge.

Weber, M. (1974) *The Protestant ethic and the spirit of capitalism*. London, Allen and Unwin.

Weber, M. (1976) *The agrarian sociology of the ancient civilizations*. London, New Left Books.

Weber, M. (1978a) *Economy and society*. 2 vols. Berkeley, University of California Press.

Weber, M. (1978b) *Selections in translation*. W. G. Runciman (ed.). Cambridge University Press.

Weber, M. (1983) *On capitalism, bureaucracy and religion*, S. Andreski (ed.). London, Allen and Unwin.

Whimster, S. and Lash, S. (eds) (1987) *Max Weber, rationality and modernity*. London, Allen and Unwin.

Wiley, N. (ed.) (1987) *The Marx–Weber debate*. Beverly Hills, Sage.

Winch, D. (1978) *Adam Smith's politics*. Cambridge University Press.

Winch, P. (1958) *The idea of a social science*. London, Routledge.

Wittfogel, K. (1957) *Oriental despotism*. New Haven, Yale University Press.

Wolf, E. (1988) 'Inventing society'. *American Ethnologist*, 15(4).

Index

Name, subjects and major concepts are indexed. All mentions of proper names are listed. In the case of concepts, indexing is restricted to the more important discussions or usages.

division of labour 15–16 27–32,
38–42, 44–7, 62–3, 65, 70–2,
76, 78, 81, 87, 94, 105, 107,
131–2, 136; *see also*
specialization
documentation 136, 138
domestic industry 36, 42, 45
domestic sphere 36–7, 126–7, 132;
see also family
Donne, J. 15
Dubček, A. viii
Durkheim, E. 1, 12, 13, 17, 18, 57,
60, 63, 65, 71, 76, 79–80, 83,
85, 88, 117, 128

Eastern Europe 146
economic determination 1–2,
56–7, 114
economy 2, 19, 28, 64, 69, 76, 82,
83, 87, 114, 116, 127, 130, 140,
142, 146
egoism 61, 71, 74, 80, 90
Egypt 148
Elias, N. 123
empowerment 2–3, 85, 131
Engels, F. 10, 114
England *see* Britain
Epicurus 18
equality 59–60, 66, 74, 75, 84, 85,
87–9, 105, 128, 142–3
Equal Rights Amendment 85
estate *see Stand*
ethic of responsibility 147, 150, 151
ethical dualism 115, 119, 123
ethical neutrality 150
ethnicity 49, 81, 103–4
ethos 3, 75, 80, 95, 96, 100, 104,
113–16, 119–33 *passim*, 137–8,
150; *see also* morality, spirit of
capitalism
examinations 79, 137
exchange value 23, 25–30, 64,
66–7, 87–8

factory 41–5, 50–1, 98, 115, 135,
144

Factory Acts 39, 85
family 10, 31, 33, 36, 39, 55, 68,
75, 84–5, 89, 99, 127, 131,
139–40
fetishism 61–2, 64, 89
feudalism 10, 16, 18, 32, 34, 49,
53, 68, 75–8, 87, 108, 111, 132,
137, 142, 145; *see also*
medieval society, serfdom
force 34–5, 59, 68, 76, 80, 83, 94,
100, 103, 129, 141
formal rationality 96, 98, 119
formal subordination of labour to
capital 38, 99
Foucault, M. x, 1, 39, 63, 78, 80,
85, 120, 122, 123–4, 131
France 76, 80–1, 145; *see also*
French Revolution
Frank, A.G. 47
Franklin, B. 130
free labour 12, 24, 33–4, 37, 49,
88–9, 94–5, 98–9, 105, 106; *see
also* wage labour, working class
freedom 14, 28, 55, 59–61, 65–6,
70, 73–5, 89, 95, 98–100, 103,
126
French Revolution 4, 7, 11, 152
Freud, S. 120
Frisby, D. 1, 46, 106, 148

gender relations 5, 31–2, 36–7, 49,
54, 58, 68, 69, 74, 84–6, 88, 99,
108, 123, 126–7, 129, 132, 139
geomancy 115
Germany 22, 49, 78, 152
Giddens, A. 12, 15, 68
globalization 2, 10–12, 47, 53–5,
63, 87, 109, 134, 137
Godelier, M. 69
Goethe, W. von 152
Greece 22, 110, 118, 150; *see also*
ancient society

habit 39, 51, 96, 114, 123, 136
handicrafts 15, 38, 40–2, 47, 50
Havel, V. viii–ix